Ken Jaffe Leslie Falconer

Create inspiring activity areas for young children using found objects or recycled materials.

7243 Scotchwood Lane, Grawn MI 49637

www.mothergoosetime.com

Ken Jaffe & Leslie Falconer
Straw into Gold: create inspiring activity areas for young children using found objects or recycled materials.

ISBN: 9780983039006

Acknowledgements

ICRI and Mother Goose Time are deeply indebted to many children's experts around the world for the development of Straw into Gold. All of these individuals or groups are part of our extended family.

More than 10 years ago our work with early childhood development in the slums of Guayaquil, Ecuador first showed us programs where we saw amazing use of found objects transformed by energetic teachers and parents into meaningful children's activities. Since then, we have also worked with early childhood professionals in more than 30 countries to help them to see what was around them that could be utilized to develop exciting, stimulating, developmentally appropriate activities which can assist in enabling children to grow and thrive in refugee camps, in areas with little water or sanitation or in areas where children have a bounty of possibilities.

Many thanks to our ICRI Zimbabwe team, Rufaro Kangai, Country Director, Monica Mhondiwa and Stella Satiya, Educators/Field Representatives at our Marondera center for their tremendous on the ground work with AIDS orphans, creating amazing activities for young children under very difficult conditions, and for their contribution to this book. They have truly turned straw into gold.

We are particularly grateful to our staff at our Hearts Leap model early childhood centers in Northern California where a number of ICRI staff made a great impact on this book. Those staff include, Ellie Mashhour, our remarkable Child Care Operations Manager who is also a skilled ECD trainer at our Africa programs and Nancy Hughes, Chris Taaffe, Jude Sapp, Sarah Poh, Gretchen Stites, Claudia Campazzo, Yanci Lucero, Anthea Peck, Jeannde Bertero, Michelle Krigbaum, and Adrian Villegas

Great thanks go out to Leslie Capello and Chou Nuon for their contribution. Olga Cordoba for her illustrations and book layout design.

We see this book as a beginning in the efforts to help children to experience the joy of early childhood. Your feedback, comments and ideas for new activities or variations presented here will always be welcomed. We look forward to adding to this publication in the future with your activities included.

With great hope for all young children,

Ken Jaffe
ICRI

Leslie Falconer
Mother Goose Time, Inc.

Table of Contents

Why This Book?

Teachers and children around the world often lack even the basic materials, which can be assembled into activities to provide stimulation, growth and development. All of the activities in this book are made with materials that can be found locally or can be adapted by you, using materials you may have where you live or work. These activities are intended to cost very little to nothing.

This book can be used in all types of early childhood settings including childcare centers, in home child care, orphanages, refugee camps, group homes, rural preschools, pre-primary or primary schools. The activities can be set up anywhere: on the ground; in a room with dirt, cement, wood, carpet or vinyl floors; in a place that has been built as an early childhood center; or in a place that no one thought would ever be used by children.

Teachers, school leaders, parents, volunteers, community members and children can use this book as a guide to creating wonderful, stimulating activities for young children.

The activities you create can be grouped into activity areas. Activity areas allow children the freedom to explore their senses, imaginations and creativity. This book will show you how to make many activities that can be divided into areas such as those listed below.

Children learn best when they can move, touch and explore throughout the day. Carefully designed activity areas allow children to develop important cognitive, social/emotional and physical skills. Use the room map on the following page as a guide or suggestion to setting up your own activity areas.

- Art
- Music and Movement
- Block and Wheel Toy
- Manipulatives
- Dramatic Play
- Reading/Writing
- Math
- Science

This plan is one suggestion for setting up your room to include activity areas as suggested in this book.

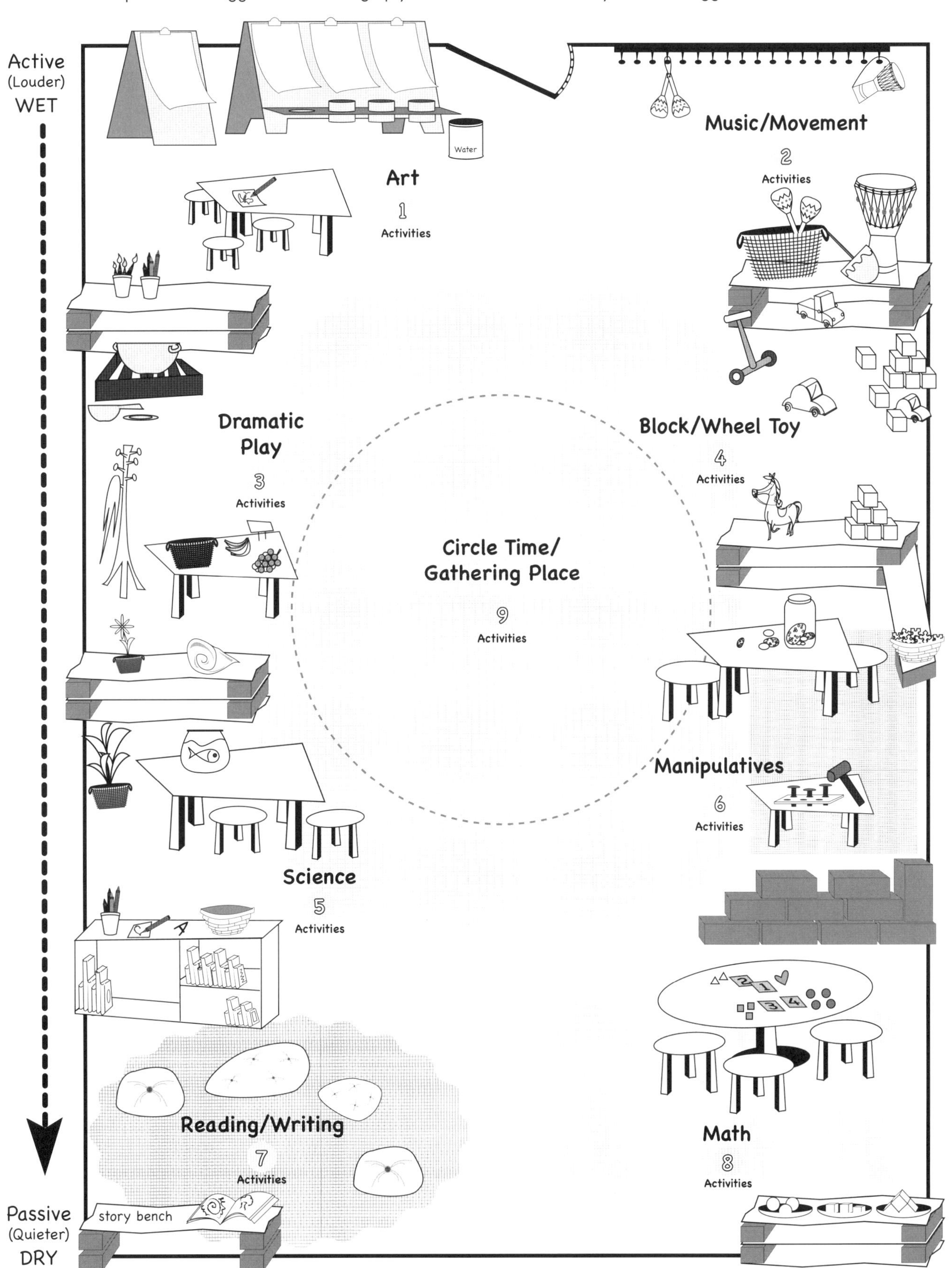

Straw-Blown Painting

Art

Area in which this activity would be found.

Skills

- Fine motor
- Creativity

Materials

- ☐ Paper
- ☐ Straws (or cupped hands)
- ☐ Water
- ☐ Paint or crushed berries
- ☐ Spoon

Activity Description

- Add water to your paint so that the paint turns into a thin liquid (like watercolor paints).
- Using a spoon, make a puddle of paint in the center of your paper.
- Use a straw (or make a tunnel with your hand) to blow the paint around the surface of the paper.
- Before the paint dries, add another color. Let the paint overlap and blend. Try blowing your paint from one corner or out from the center.

Marble Painting

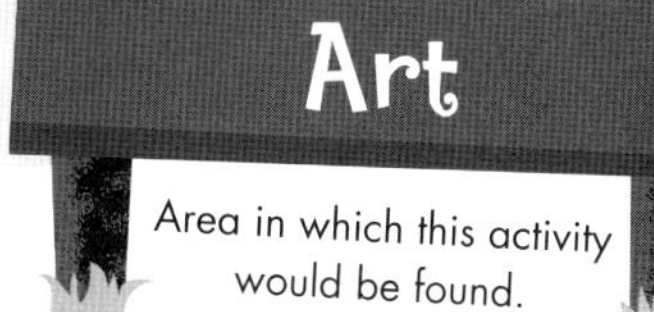

Skills
- Motor control
- Hand-eye coordination

Materials
- ☐ A shallow box or box lid
- ☐ Paper
- ☐ Paint
- ☐ Marbles or round stones

Activity Description
- Place a piece of paper in the bottom of box.
- Dip marbles or stones into the paint and then place into the box.
- Twist, wiggle, and twirl the box around to make designs—the marble or stone is your paintbrush!

1 Find Supplies **2 Make and Play**

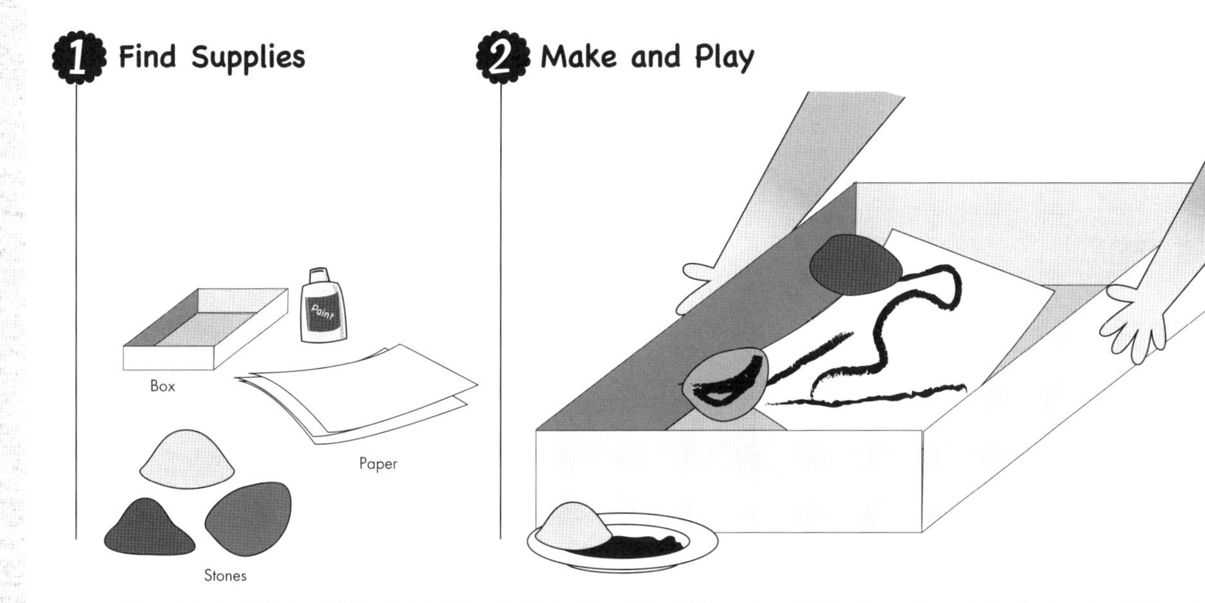

Splatter Prints

Art

Area in which this activity would be found.

Skills

- Fine motor
- Creativity
- Spatial relationships

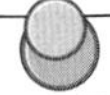

Materials

- ☐ Paper or Cardboard
- ☐ Paint brush, old toothbrush, or spray bottle
- ☐ Paint or water
- ☐ Items to outline (cut pieces of cardboard, leaves, etc.)

Activity Description

- Place an item, such as a leaf, onto a piece of paper on a level surface.
- Using a stiff paintbrush, toothbrush, or a spray bottle, spray water or paint all around the leaf.
- Remove the leaf and see the leaf shape surrounded by the splattered paint. Try using more than one object to create new designs on the paper. (For example, use 4 leaves to create a butterfly!)

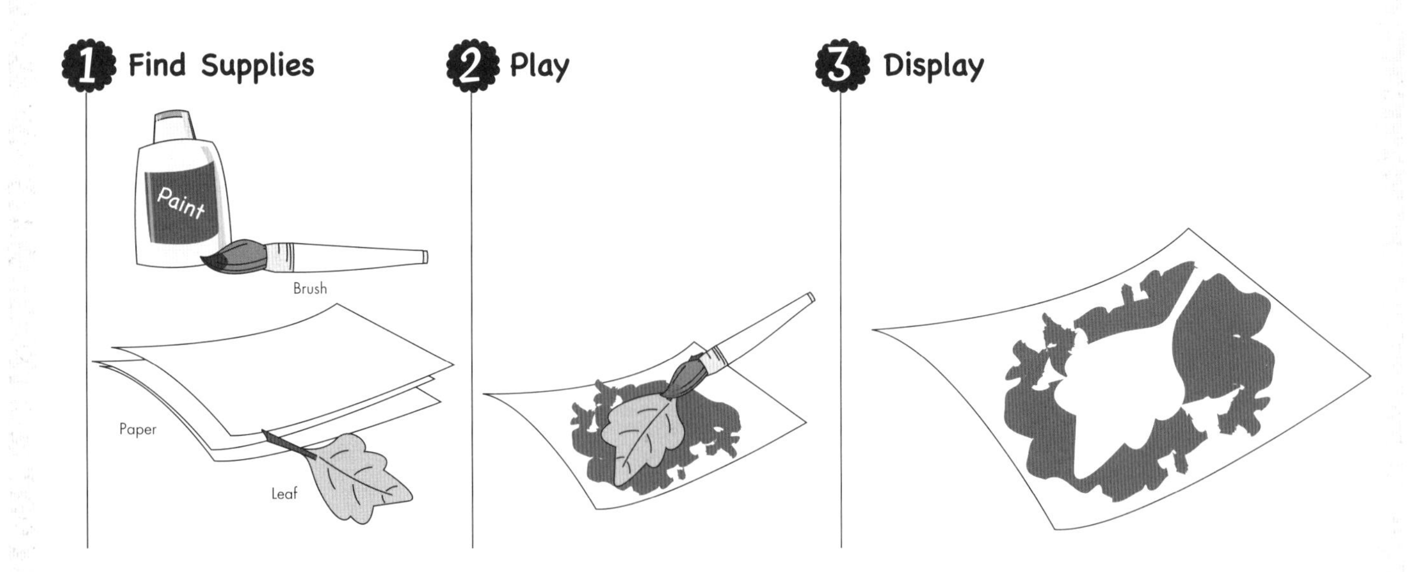

Continuous Picture

Skills
- Fine motor
- Drawing

Materials
- ☐ Paper
- ☐ Something to write with

Activity Description
- Draw a picture on a piece of paper, but don't lift up the pencil as you draw.
- Make a picture with one long, continuous line.
- Try drawing people this way, or an imaginary animal!

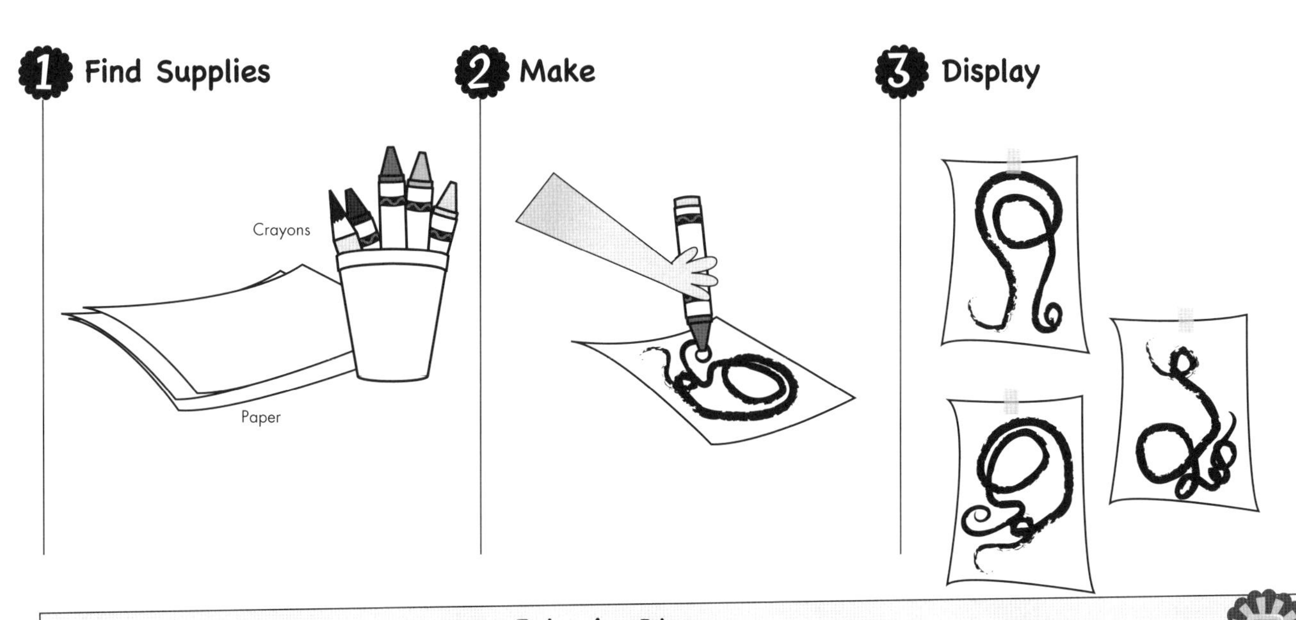

Extension Idea

Sing a song together and invite children to make a "continuous music picture". At the end of the song, take turns showing the pictures.

Rubbings

Art

Area in which this activity would be found.

Skills

- Spatial awareness
- Fine motor control

Materials

- ❑ Paper or cardboard
- ❑ Leaves, small sticks, flat, stones
- ❑ Crayon or something to write with

Activity Description

- Place a piece of paper over some leaves.
- Rub a crayon back and forth over the paper to show the texture of the leaves.
- Experiment with other textures found around the room or outside and create a texture collage.

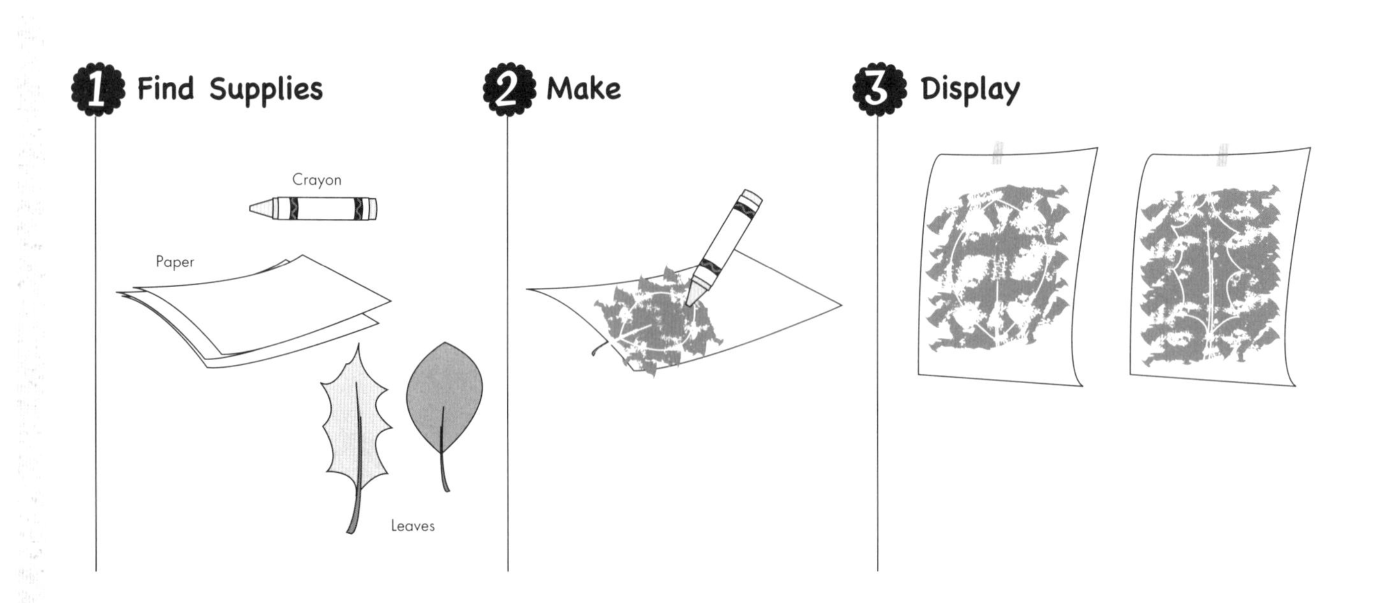

Tracing Shapes

Art

Area in which this activity would be found.

Skills

- Creativity
- Shapes
- Fine motor control

Materials

- □ Paper
- □ Something to write with (or dirt/sand surface)
- □ Cardboard
- □ Scissors

Activity Description

- Cut the cardboard into multiple sizes of circles, triangles and squares.
- Children choose one shape and trace around the various sizes on paper or in dirt to create a design or picture.
- Discuss which shapes and how many were used.

3 Display

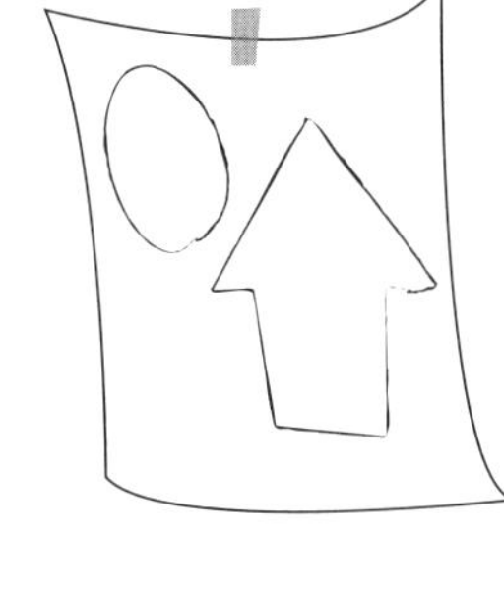

Stamping

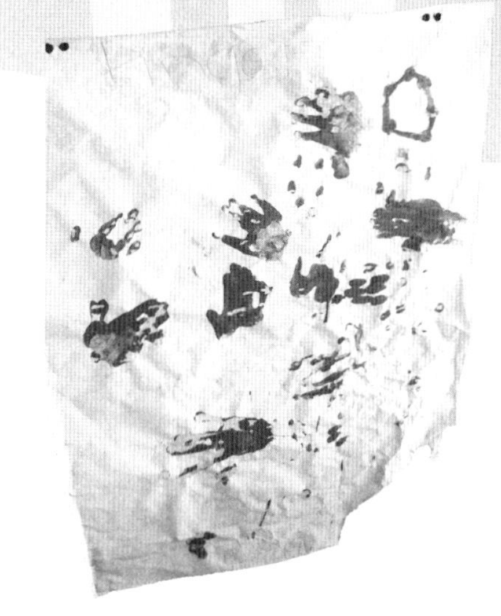

Art
Area in which this activity would be found.

Skills
- Spatial awareness
- Fine motor

Materials
- ❑ Bowl
- ❑ Grass tied together
- ❑ Bottle caps or sponges
- ❑ Flat surface (paper, cloth)
- ❑ Paint or plant die

Activity Description
- Mix paint and water in a bowl.
- Children experiment by dipping the object (grass, sponge) into the paint then stamp or sweep onto the flat surface to create unique designs
- Use one surface for all children to paint on or individual pieces of material for each child to paint on

1 Make or Find Supplies

2 Set Up and Play

Note: Have children paint together on one cloth or material, and then hang on the wall at the children's eye level. This is a great cooperative art project that builds a sense of community.

Community Works of Art

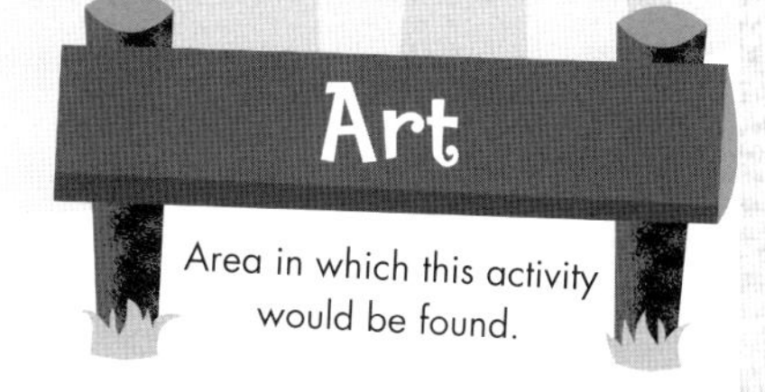

Skills
- Creativity
- Cooperation
- Collaboration
- Fine motor skills

Materials
- ☐ One large piece of cloth, paper, cardboard, end of a box or canvas
- ☐ Paint, mud, local plant dyes or other available materials to paint and draw with

Activity Description
- Children and teacher discuss what type of art project they could all make together.
- Children discuss how they will develop the community art project and may make small sketches.
- Children utilize paint, mud, local plant dyes, or other available materials to create a painting , drawing, or sculpture.
- Display the group art.

Wire Sculpture

Art

Area in which this activity would be found.

Skills

- Fine Motor
- Reasoning
- Creative expression

Materials

- ☐ Bendable wire (approximately 3 inches long)
- ☐ Beads
- ☐ Wood pieces
- ☐ Bottle caps
- ☐ Sticks

Activity Description

- Set wire, beads, wood pieces, bottle caps and sticks in the center of a table.
- Children manipulate and experiment by bending the wire.
- Children create a creative sculpture using the materials.
- Display sculptures on shelves or a table.

1 Make or Find Supplies **2 Set Up** **3 Create**

Did you know?

Children in Kenya make elaborate cars with moveable parts from wire, called Galimotos.

Toss and Catch

Skills

- Gross motor
- Peer interaction

Materials

- ☐ Ball or ball type object (tied rope or sisal, cloth, small sewn pillow)
- ☐ Basket or bucket

Activity Description

- Set out balls, baskets, or buckets.
- Children may toss, catch, or roll the balls.
- Encourage children to play with a friend and have them make up ball games.

Balance Obstacle Course

Skills
- Balancing
- Climbing
- Jumping
- Gross Motor Development

Materials
- ☐ Blanket or large leaves
- ☐ Chair
- ☐ Wood piece or cardboard

Activity Description
- Work together with the children to set up an obstacle course.
- Leave the obstacle course set up for the day.
- The next day, encourage children to rearrange and set up a new obstacle course.

1 Find Supplies **2 Set Up and Play**

Pounding Musician

Skills
- Auditory discrimination
- Rhythm
- Gross motor

Materials
- ☐ Buckets, bowls, or pans
- ☐ Sticks
- ☐ Wood branches/wood pieces tied together
- ☐ Water or Liquid

Activity Description

- Children choose an object to pound with (stick, wood branches/wood pieces, or their hand.)
- Children create drums with plastic buckets, bowls, or boxes.
- Children set up their drums and play!
- Pour water in some of the containers to change the sound.
- Ask: How do these drums sound differently. What kind of song do you like to play?

Make Your Own Dance

Skills

- Seriation
- Gross motor development
- Creativity

Materials

- ☐ Instruments (home made)
- ☐ Found objects (to dance with)

Activity Description

- Children use their own cultural knowledge to make dance steps relevant to their own family, tradition or national dance culture.
- Children create each dance step and teachers assist and record steps.
- Children perform dances and share with other groups of children.

1 Make or Find Supplies

2 Set Up and Dance

Bottle Cap Music Makers

Skills

- Small motor development
- Use of local or found objects
- Creativity in development of musical instrument

Materials

- ☐ Stiff wire
- ☐ Bottle caps
- ☐ Sharp object

Activity Description

- Adult uses a sharp object to create a hole in each bottle cap.
- Children thread bottle caps onto stiff wire.
- Bend the wire closed into a circle.
- Children use the bottle cap music maker to create rhythms and to use in the development of dances and other movement.

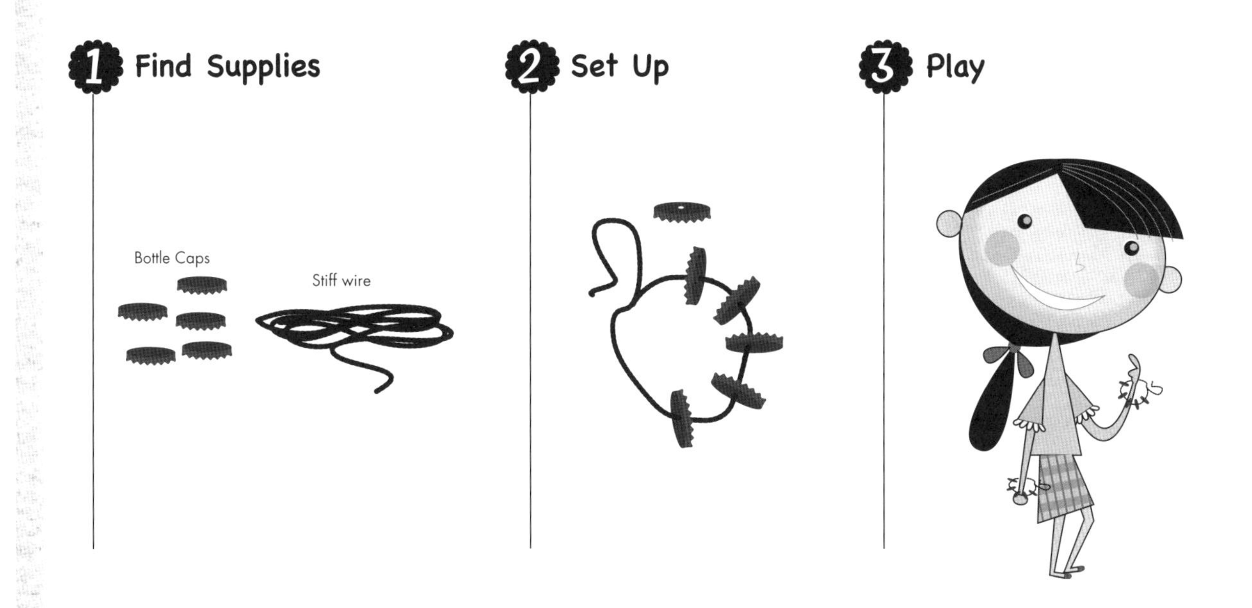

Jump Over

Skills

- Body Coordination
- Critical Thinking

Materials
- ☐ Pillows
- ☐ Boxes

Activity Description

- Set pillows or boxes in the music and movement area.
- Children build a small tower and practice jumping over it.
- Children continue to add objects on top of the tower and take turns jumping.
- Encourage some children to play music while other children play the jumping game.

1 Make or Find Supplies

2 Set Up and Play

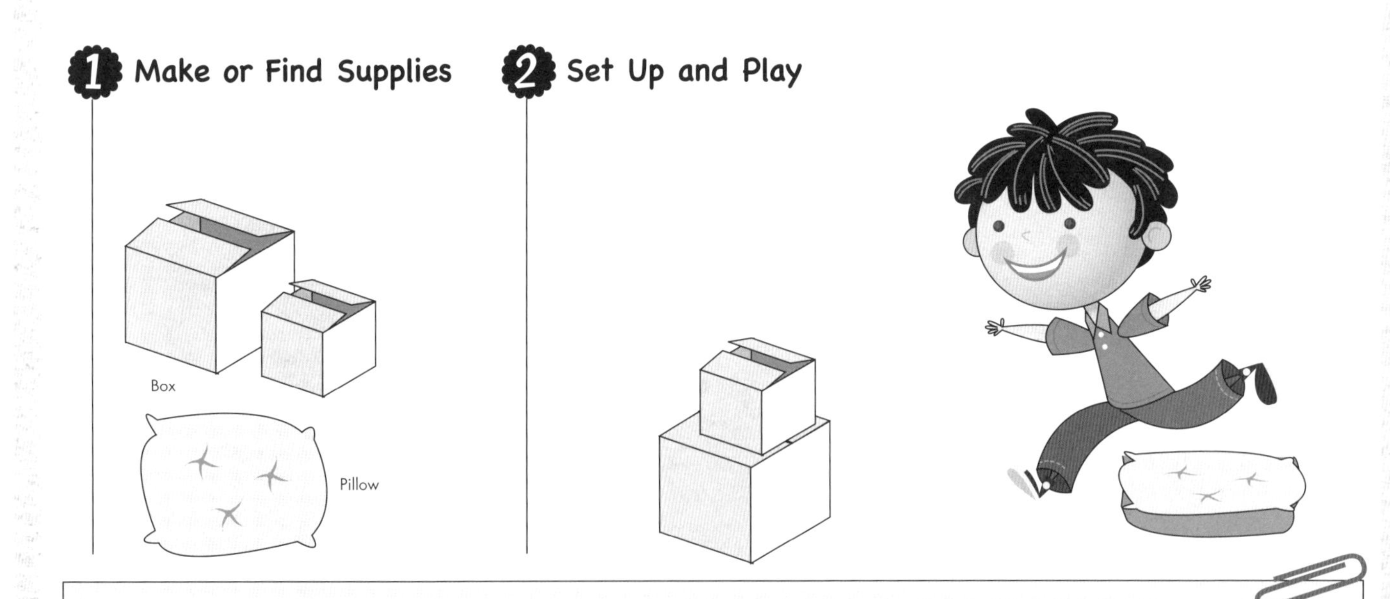

Note: Set up in a safe place where children will be safe to fall.

Homemade Shakers

Skills

- Small and gross motor coordination
- Creativity

Materials
- ☐ Soda pop cans
- ☐ Pebbles
- ☐ Sticks

Activity Description

- Children take pebbles and place inside soda can.
- Push a thick stick into opening of soda can, creating a strong and permanent seal.

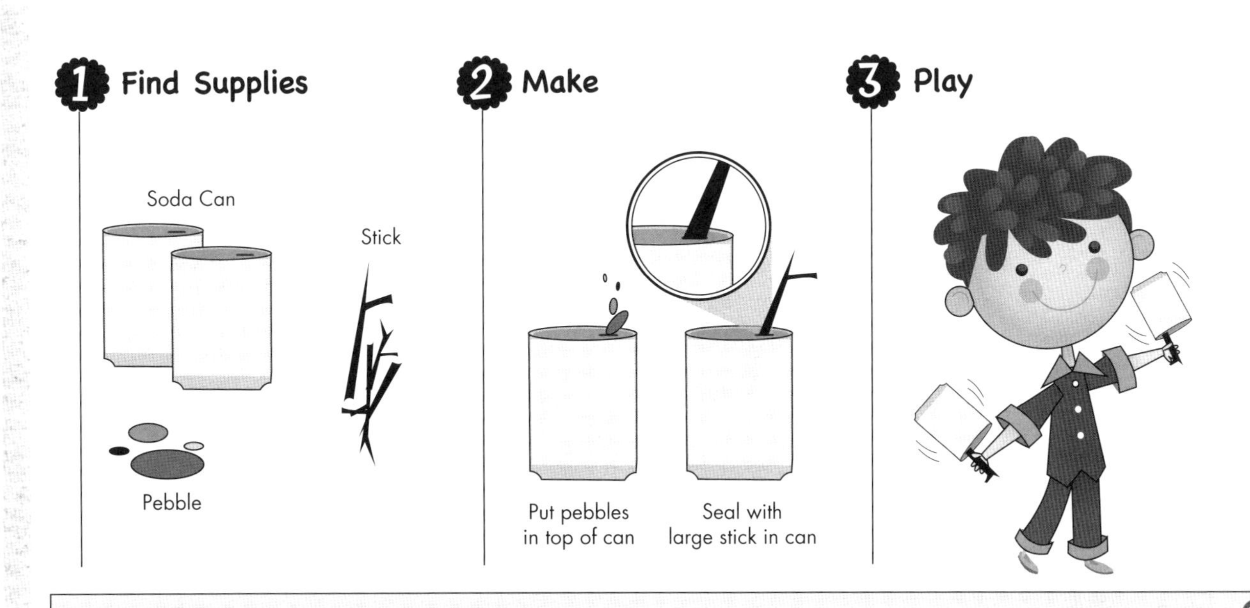

Note: Remove the tabs from the can. Observe and monitor safe play. Child should not eat pebbles.

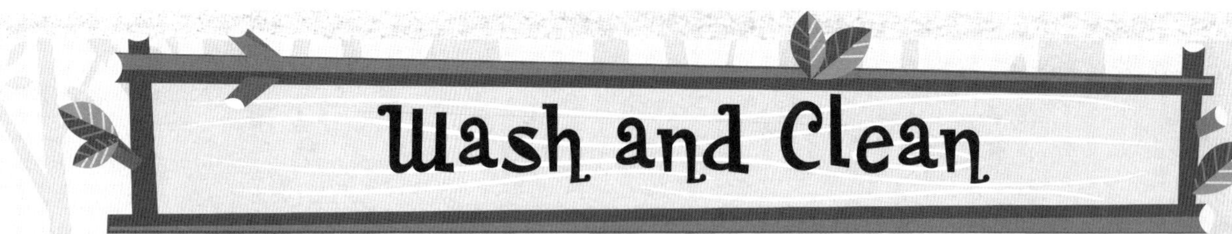

Wash and Clean

Dramatic Play

Area in which this activity would be found.

Skills

- Role-playing
- Language development

Materials

- ☐ Cotton cloth pieces
- ☐ 3 large bowls or buckets half full with water
- ☐ Objects for wiping and washing (clean plastic containers, plastic baskets, wood bowls, plastic or wood dolls or animals)

Activity Description

- Children choose an object and wash it.
- Children share the cotton cloths and take turns dipping them in water, and wiping clean the objects.
- Children set out the objects to dry

1 Find Supplies

Cloth

Objects

Bucket with water

2 Set Up and Play

Extension Idea

Create an area for hanging wet cloth pieces out to dry (rope pulled between 2 chairs and fastened at each end or hang on backs of chairs).

Market

Dramatic Play

Area in which this activity would be found.

Skills

- Creative thinking
- Social-emotional
- Language development

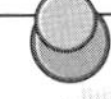

Materials

- ☐ Variety of supplies and objects representing the market place (such as baskets, small tables, cloth/material, bowls, recycled or empty food boxes and cans, leaves to represent money)
- ☐ Cardboard pieces for signs
- ☐ Writing instruments

Activity Description

- Children and teacher work together to make store supplies such as For Sale signs, play money and store products.
- Children set up store.
- Children make-believe shopping and selling.

1 Make or Find Supplies

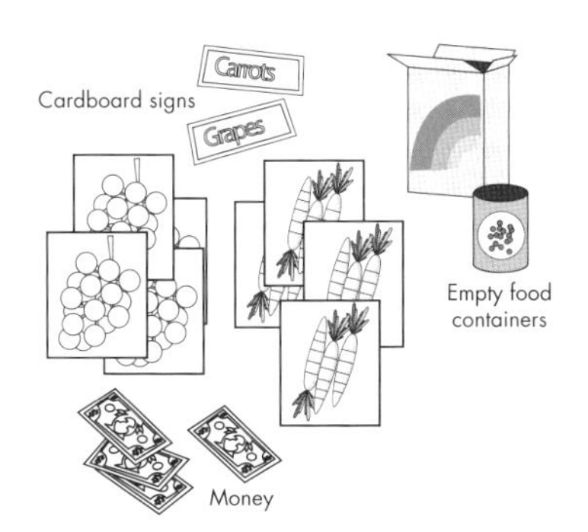

2 Set Up

3 Play

In the Kitchen

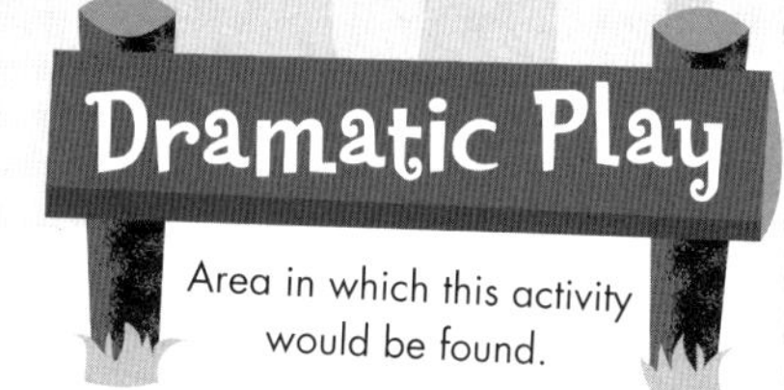

Skills

- Creative thinking
- Language development
- Dramatic play

Materials

- ❑ Old box for stove
- ❑ Sticks
- ❑ Leaves, pebbles and dirt for cooking ingredients
- ❑ Old or used bowls or pots
- ❑ Cardboard to cut out fake fruit, vegetables or fish

Activity Description

- Children and teacher make kitchen supplies.
- Children set up their kitchen.
- Children make-believe cooking and serving food.

What Am I?

Dramatic play

Area in which this activity would be found.

Skills
- Creativity
- Memory
- Group cooperation and interaction

Materials
- ❑ Old clothing, cloth pieces, hats, adult shoes or other materials

Activity Description

- Child dresses in dramatic play area in dress-up clothing.
- Ask other children what they think he or she is.
- The children attempt to guess what the child is portraying.
- The winning guess receives a hug from the child who is asking the question.

1 Find Supplies

2 Dress Up and Guess

Make A Clinic

Dramatic Play

Area in which this activity would be found.

Skills

- Creativity
- Language development
- Memory
- Cooperation

Materials

- ☐ Blanket or towel
- ☐ Paper
- ☐ Empty plastic bottles
- ☐ Strips of cloth

Activity Description

- Gather supplies and then set them in the dramatic play area.
- Children take turns pretending to be the patient or the doctor.

Over, Under, and Through

Block/Wheel Toy

Area in which this activity would be found.

Skills

- Spatial awareness
- Fine motor
- Critical thinking

Materials

- ☐ Blocks
- ☐ Wheel toys
- ☐ Thick sticks
- ☐ Stones
- ☐ Empty plastic bottles
- ☐ Small pieces of cloth
- ☐ Cardboard boxes or pieces
- ☐ Wire

Activity Description

- Cut both ends off the plastic bottles to make tubes. Lay all supplies in the corner of a room or on a shelf.
- Children create rolling objects, tunnels, bridges or roads.
- Children push or roll stones through tunnels and roads.

Stacking Boxes

Block/Wheel Toy

Area in which this activity would be found.

Skills

- Critical thinking
- Creative expression
- Dramatic play

Materials

- ☐ Small boxes
- ☐ Medium boxes
- ☐ Large boxes

Activity Description

- Set out boxes in activity area.
- Children stack and line up boxes to create walls, tunnels, mazes, houses.
- Allow children to add toys and other objects to extend play.

1 Find Supplies

2 Play

Cars and Trucks

Block/Wheel Toy

Area in which this activity would be found.

Skills

- Critical thinking
- Creativity
- Role playing

Materials

- ☐ Wood blocks or small cardboard boxes
- ☐ Materials for drawing or painting
- ☐ Scissors
- ☐ Tape

Activity Description

- Children cut holes for windows and doors out of small cardboard cartons or boxes.
- Children paint or draw a car-like or truck-like designs onto the cardboard boxes.

1 Find Supplies

2 Play

Extension Idea

Try making small wheels out of cardboard and then attaching to car with wire or straw. Attach a string at the front of the car and use as a pull toy.

Wheels of All Kind

Block/Wheel Toy

Area in which this activity would be found.

Skills

- Small motor development
- Creativity
- Problem solving

Materials

- ❑ Wire, cardboard, wood or other materials that can be molded or modeled
- ❑ Scissors

Activity Description

- Children make wheels out of wire, wood, clay, paper, mud, cans or other cylinders.
- Children roll and maneuver the wheels in various manners.
- Store all wheels in the wheel and block toy area of the room.

1 Make and Find Supplies

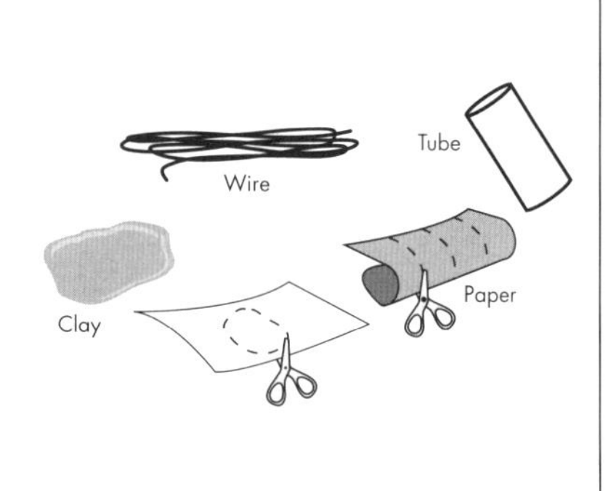

2 Play

Optional: Find and use motorcycle tires with a stick to roll down the early childhood center length or in an outdoor area nearby.

Blocks From Almost Nothing

Block/Wheel Toy

Area in which this activity would be found.

Skills

- Small and gross motor development
- Problem solving
- Creativity

Materials

- ☐ Cardboard boxes, wood blocks, or other similar materials that are found or locally made.
- ☐ Scissors
- ☐ Tape

Activity Description

- Fold cardboard or paper into block shapes.
- Tape block side to reinforce.
- Paint or color boxes.
- Within the block and wheel toy area, children display their blocks and create buildings. This supports creative and imaginative play.

1 Make or Find Supplies

2 Set Up

3 Play

Disappearing Water

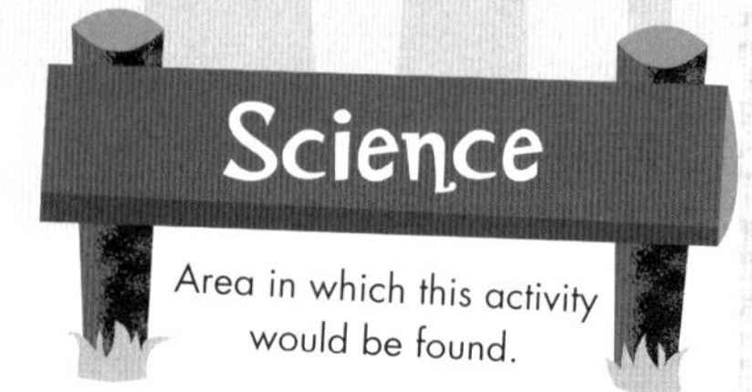

Skills

- Cognitive development
- Reasoning

Materials
- ☐ Water
- ☐ Wood or cardboard

Activity Description

- Children pour a small amount of water on both pieces of wood or cardboard.
- Children taken turns fanning one of the pieces of wood.
- Children observe and discuss what they think is happening. Which piece is drying faster? What is the wind from fanning doing?

Watch it Sprout

Science

Area in which this activity would be found.

Skills

- Concepts of change
- Observation

Materials

- ❑ Cups
- ❑ Water
- ❑ Bean or other seeds
- ❑ Paper
- ❑ Something to write with

Activity Description

- Children pour a small amount of water into a small bowl or cup.
- Place a bean inside the water and set aside.
- Children visit their bean daily and observe what happens.
- Leave paper and drawing materials next to the beans so that children can draw or write about their observations.
- Hang the drawings on the walls.

1 Find Supplies

2 Set Up and Observe

Blowing Experiment

Skills
- Cognitive development
- Reasoning

Materials
- ☐ Sticks for measuring
- ☐ Leaves or feathers
- ☐ Basket

Activity Description
- Put the leaves, feathers, or other light objects in basket.
- Children choose an object, place it on the floor or table and blow as hard as they can on the object.
- Children watch the object move and then measure how many stick lengths they were able to blow it.

Where Does the Water Go?

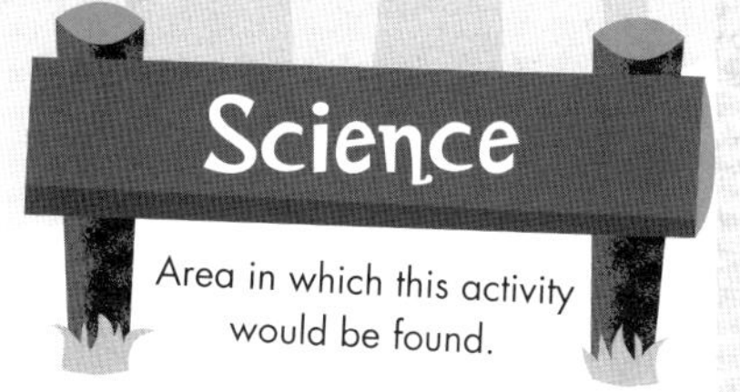

Skills
- Cognitive development
- Reasoning
- Scientific Theory

Materials
- ❑ Small open container
- ❑ Something to write with
- ❑ Water or liquid

Activity Description
- Teacher and children find a small container and fill with any kind of water or liquid.
- Make a mark at the water line.
- Leave the container in a safe place in the science area.
- Children observe that the water is disappearing.
- Each day, mark the new water line.
- Teachers and children discuss evaporation (water going into the air).

Extension Idea

Leave a different marked empty container outside in a safe place. After a rain shower, children can measure the amount of rain that has fallen.

Amazing Balancing Stick

Science

Area in which this activity would be found.

Skills

- Hand-eye coordination/fine motor
- Critical thinking

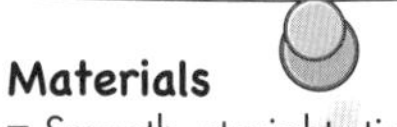

Materials

- ☐ Smooth, straight stick
- ☐ Bucket

Activity Description

- Put a collection of smooth, straight sticks in a bucket.
- Children choose a stick and try balancing it on their finger or between two hands.
- Encourage children to find the middle of the stick and try placing their finger at the center point.
- Discuss which stick is easiest and hardest to balance.

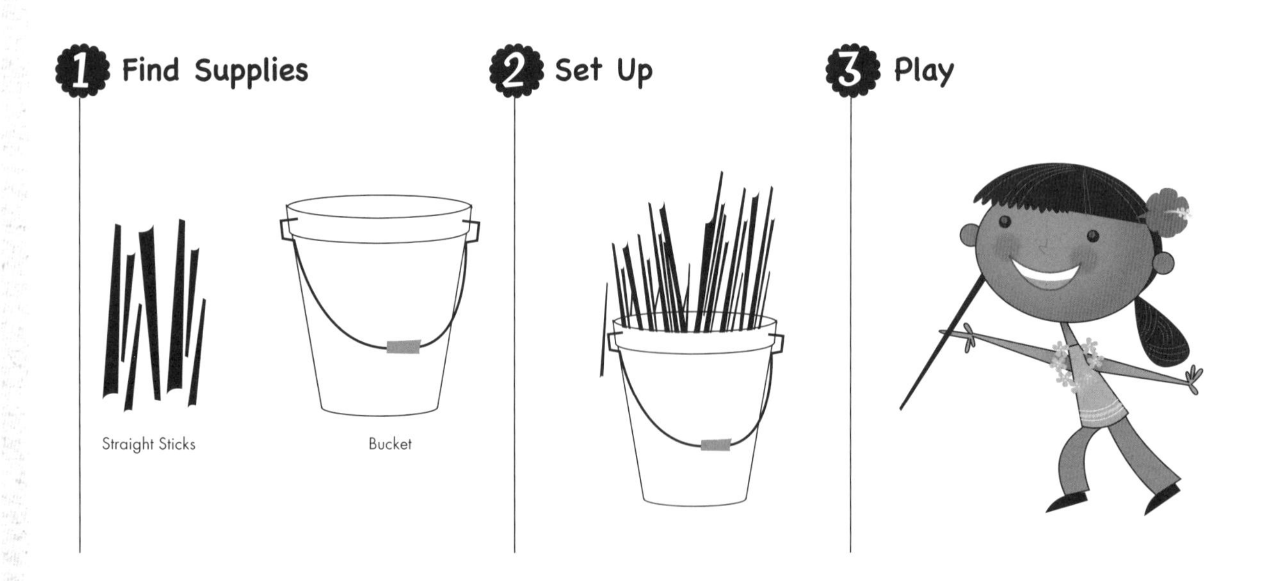

Racing Sticks

Science

Area in which this activity would be found.

Skills
- Observation
- Prediction

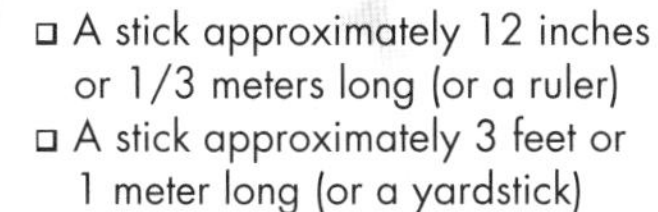

Materials
- ☐ A stick approximately 12 inches or 1/3 meters long (or a ruler)
- ☐ A stick approximately 3 feet or 1 meter long (or a yardstick)

Activity Description

- Children stand up both the tall and short sticks and steady each of them with just the finger tip.
- Children guess which stick will fall first to the ground.
- Lean sticks forward at the same angle and let go of the sticks at the same time.
- Observe as the shortest stick always falls first.
- Allow children to experiment with the stick races throughout the day.
- Later in the day, ask students what they observed. Explain the shortest stick has a lower center of balance. The taller the object, the longer it will take to fall and hit the ground.

1 Find Supplies

2 Hold

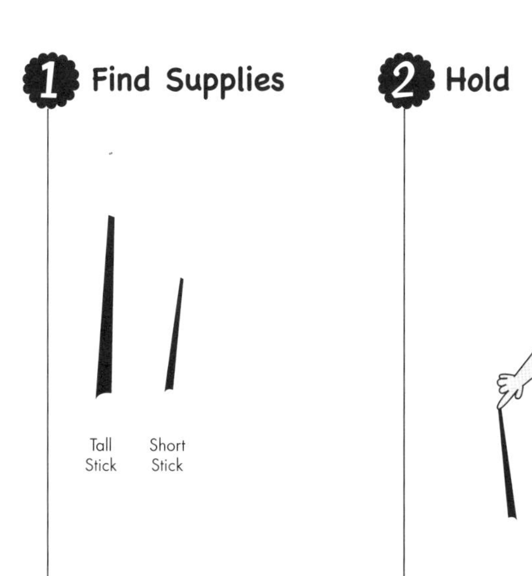

3 Drop

Great Rock & Paper Race

Area in which this activity would be found.

Skills

- Observation
- Prediction
- Fine motor

Materials

- ☐ A large coin or relatively flat rock
- ☐ Paper
- ☐ Scissors

Activity Description

- Find a number of rocks or coins similar in size. Place them in a basket.
- Cut out paper circles about the same size as the rocks.
- Children choose two papers, two rocks, or a paper and a rock and then drop both items at the same time.
- Children observe which object won the dropping race.
- Ask children: how did the paper fall differently than the rock? Which fell first to the ground? Why do you think?

Did you know: Gravity is acting on both objects in the same way. However, the paper is so light that the air is able to push on it as it falls, causing it to fall more slowly. The air is not able to push hard enough on the coin to slow its fall.

Sundial Shadows

Science

Area in which this activity would be found.

Skills

- Observation
- Prediction

Materials

- ☐ A straight stick
- ☐ Stones or other markers
- ☐ A sunny day!

Activity Description

- Children find a sunny place outside and push their stick into the ground so that it is pointing straight up into the air.
- Observe where the shadow strikes the ground and place a stone along the shadow line.
- Invite children to go outside every hour, find their stick, and place a new marker along the shadow line.

Ask the children: Where do you think the next stone will be placed? Explain the earth is moving, so is our shadow.

Time in the Sun

Science

Area in which this activity would be found.

Skills
- Observation
- Prediction

Materials
- ☐ A dark colored piece of paper
- ☐ A light or white piece of paper
- ☐ A sunny day

Activity Description

- Place both a light and dark colored piece of paper in a sunny place outside.
- As the children play outside, they visit the papers to touch and determine which paper is warmer.
- Leave the papers in the sun all day, allow children to frequently touch and think about the temperature of the paper.
- Ask the Children: Which paper feels warmest? Why do you think it is warmer?

Did you know: Light colors reflect the heat from the sun, and darker colors absorb it! You can warm water this way as well, just use a dark colored cup or bowl and place it in the sunshine.

Sink or Float

Science

Area in which this activity would be found.

Skills

- Critical thinking
- Making predictions
- Observations

Materials

- ☐ Variety of objects that sink or float in water (example: sticks, stones, pebbles, leaves)
- ☐ Medium to large size bowls
- ☐ Water

Activity Description

- Fill a small bowl with water.
- Collect and place a variety of objects in a basket.
- Children place objects, one at a time, into the bowl of water to determine whether it sinks or floats.

Extension Idea

Children can sort the objects into two baskets to visually identify what happens to the object when placed in water. Baskets can be labeled with the words sink and float and/or with an illustration representing sink and float.

Mystery Texture Box

Science

Area in which this activity would be found.

Skills
- Tactile Discrimination
- Critical Thinking
- Cooperation

Materials
- ☐ Old box
- ☐ Rock
- ☐ Sock
- ☐ Stick
- ☐ Leaf
- ☐ Seed

Activity Description

- Put found objects (rock, stick, seed...) in a basket or box.
- Cut a small hole on one side of the box. The hole should be just big enough for a child to fit in his/her hand.
- Set the basket of objects and box with hole in your science area.
- Children work with a friend. One child puts an object from the basket secretly in the box.
- The other child reaches into the box and feels the object without seeing it.
- The child describes what he/she is feeling and guesses what the object is.

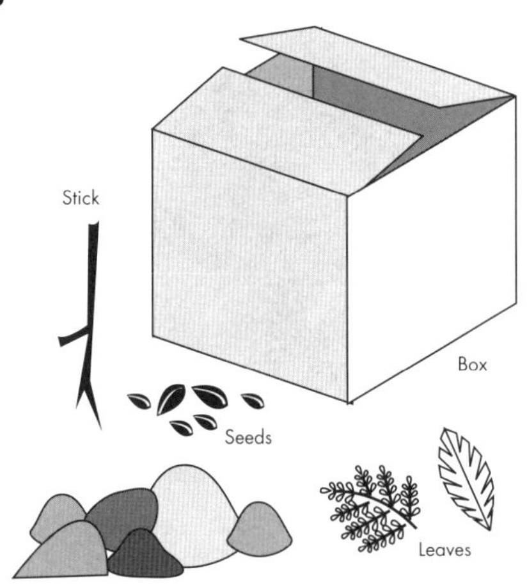

Sorting Sticks

Area in which this activity would be found.

Skills
- Critical thinking
- Color recognition
- Sorting

Materials
- ❑ 1 large box
- ❑ 3 colored baskets or small boxes
- ❑ 30 small sticks colored in groups of 10

Activity Description
- Paint or color sticks to match the colored baskets.
- Place 30 small colored sticks in a box (example: 10 red, 10 blue, 10 yellow)
- Children take one colored stick at a time from the box and place it in the matching colored basket.

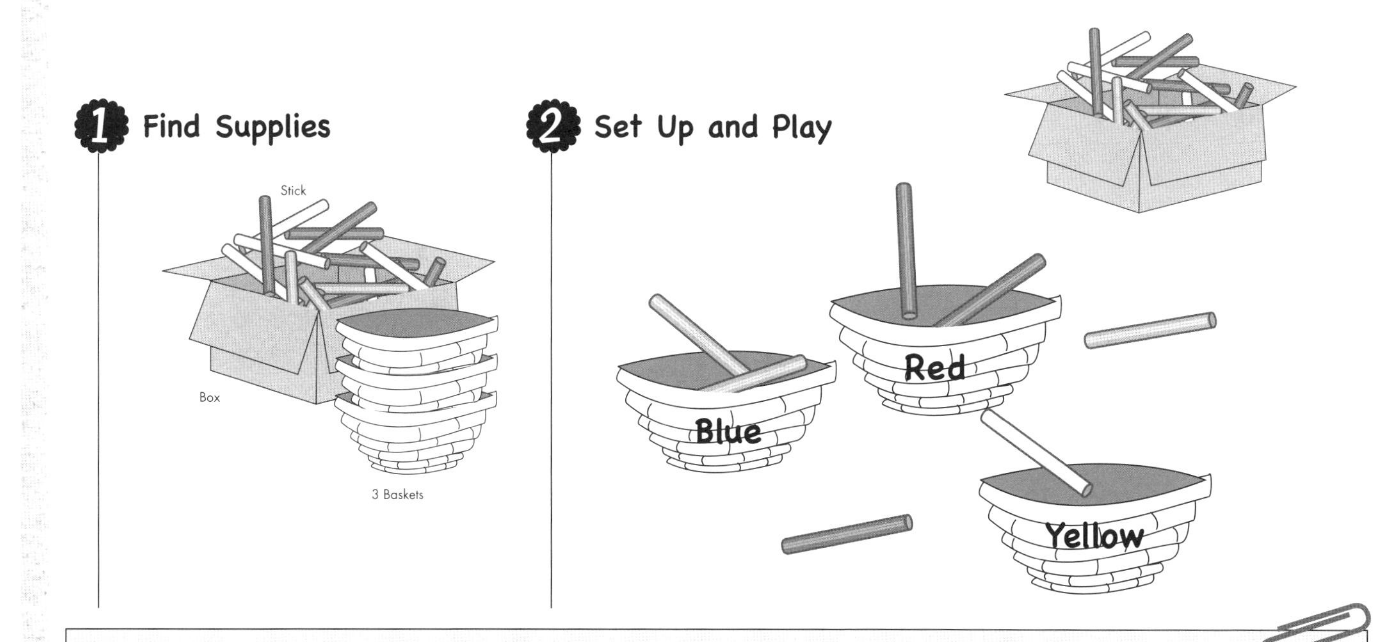

Note: Colored sticks could be chalk, crayons, found sticks from trees, etc.

Category Circles

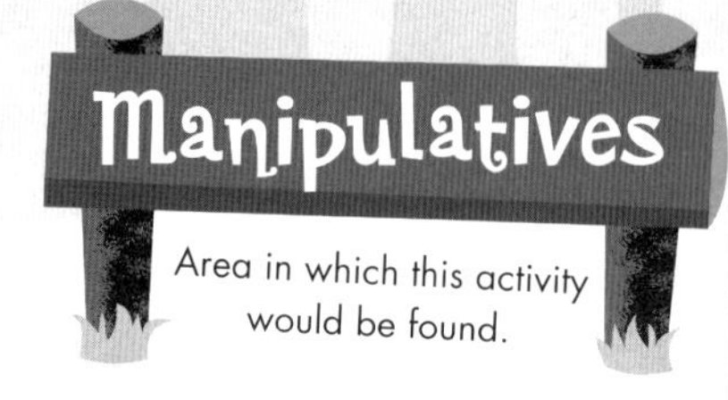

Skills

- Sorting
- Working with peers
- Logic
- Visual discrimination

Materials

- ❑ Variety of pebbles, rocks, or stones
- ❑ Large piece of paper or dirt/sand surface
- ❑ Something to write with

Activity Description

- Draw two circles on a piece of paper or in the dirt or sand. Place a pile of assorted rocks next to the circles.
- 3-4 children work together to organize stones into 2 distinctive categories (large/small or lighter/darker). Use all stones.
- Ask the children to share their categorization technique.

Extension Idea

Draw another circle on the paper or in the dirt and try sorting pebbles into three categories. Each group can discuss how they categorized their pebbles.

Threading

Skills
- Fine motor
- Eye-hand coordination

Manipulative

Area in which this activity would be found.

Materials
- ☐ Cardboard
- ☐ Pointy tool
- ☐ Thin and long strips of cloth or heavy thread

Activity Description
- Cut cardboard into long strips or simple shapes.
- With pointy tool puncture two rows of holes through cardboard, 6 holes in each row.
- Thread cloth strip through first hole and tie thick knot at the end to prevent it from pulling through the hole.
- Children can thread the cloth strip in and out of the holes in anyway they choose.

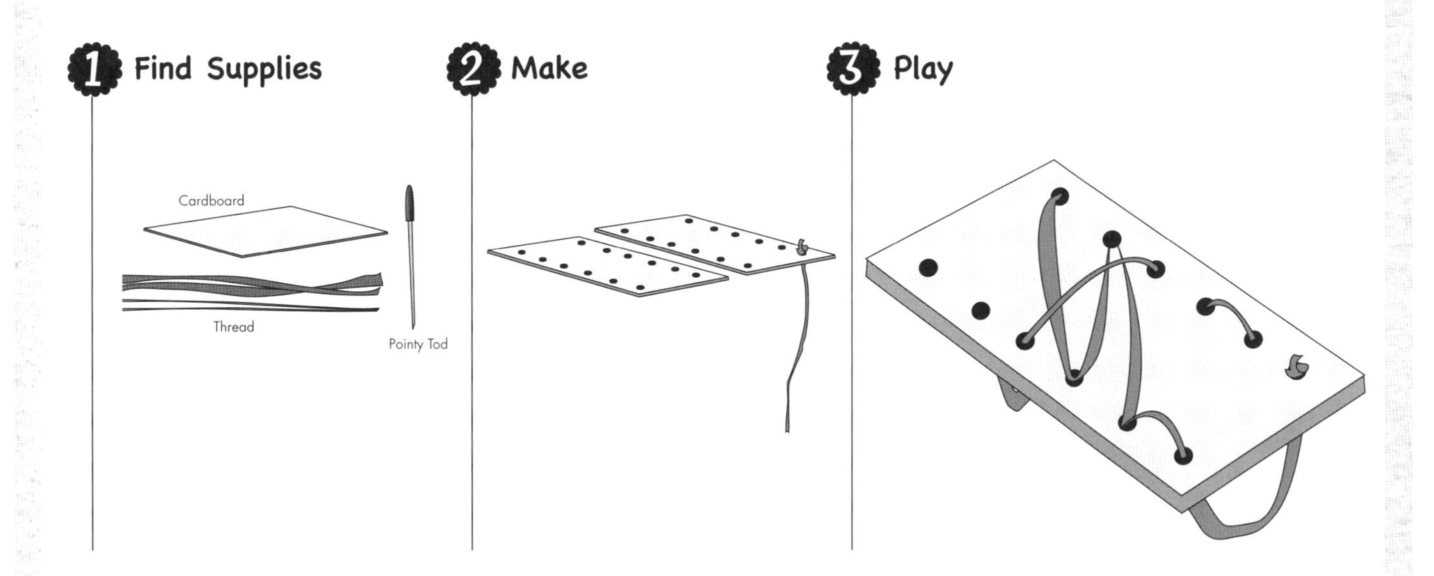

Sticks & Stones Pattern

Manipulative

Area in which this activity would be found.

Skills
- Patterning
- Fine motor

Materials
- ❑ Sticks
- ❑ Stones
- ❑ Paper or cardboard
- ❑ Something to write with

Activity Description

- Draw a variety of patterns on small pieces of paper or cardboard. (stick, stick, rock, rock or stick, rock, stick, rock)
- Set pattern cards, sticks and rocks on a table.
- Children choose one pattern card and copy the pattern, using the sticks and rocks.

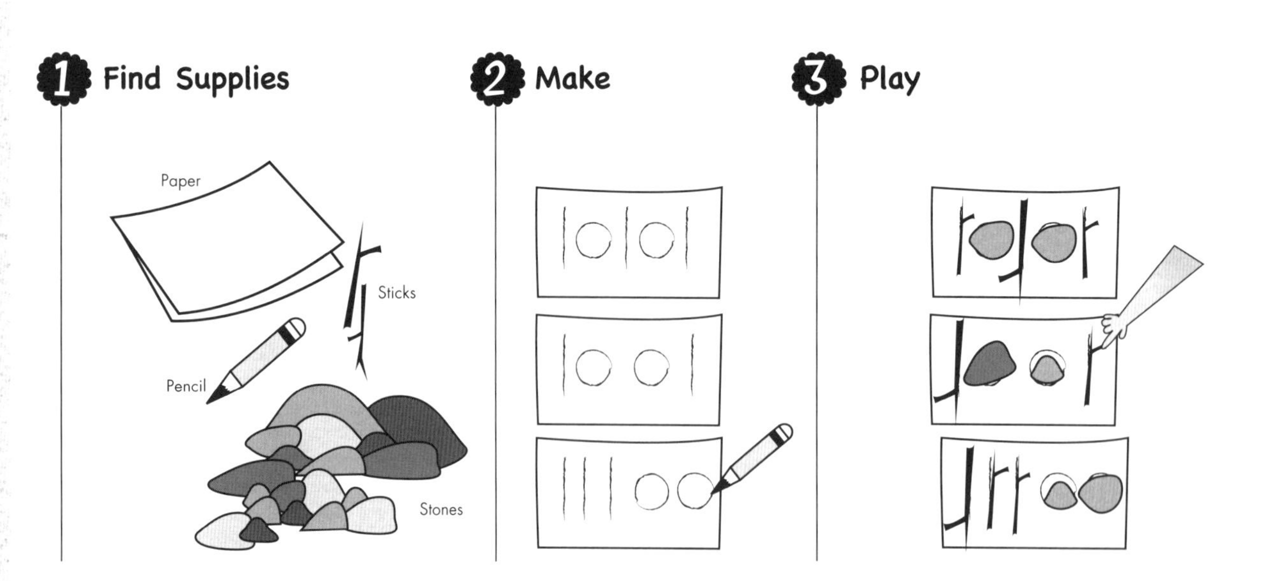

Extension Idea

Leave out blank paper and invite children to invent and draw their own patterns.

Make A Puzzle!

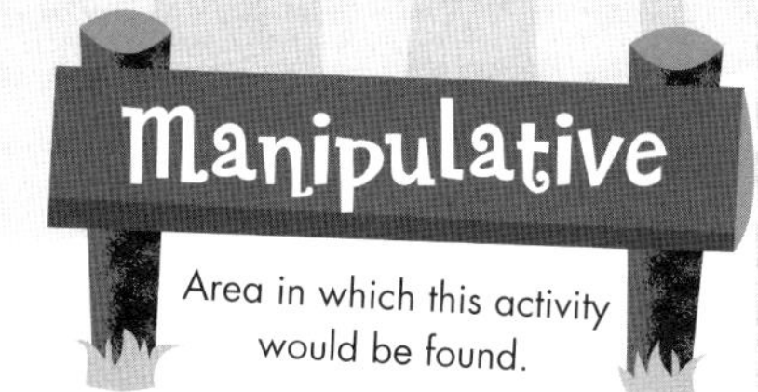

Skills
- Fine motor
- Creativity
- Critical thinking

Materials
- ❑ Cardboard
- ❑ Scissors
- ❑ Something to write with, plant die or paint

Activity Description

- Draw a picture or use one from an old magazine.
- Cut the drawing into large pieces. (4 pieces for young children. 6-12 for older children).
- Put your very own puzzle together!
- Optional: To make a more durable puzzle, glue drawing onto cardboard or an old cereal box before cutting into pieces.

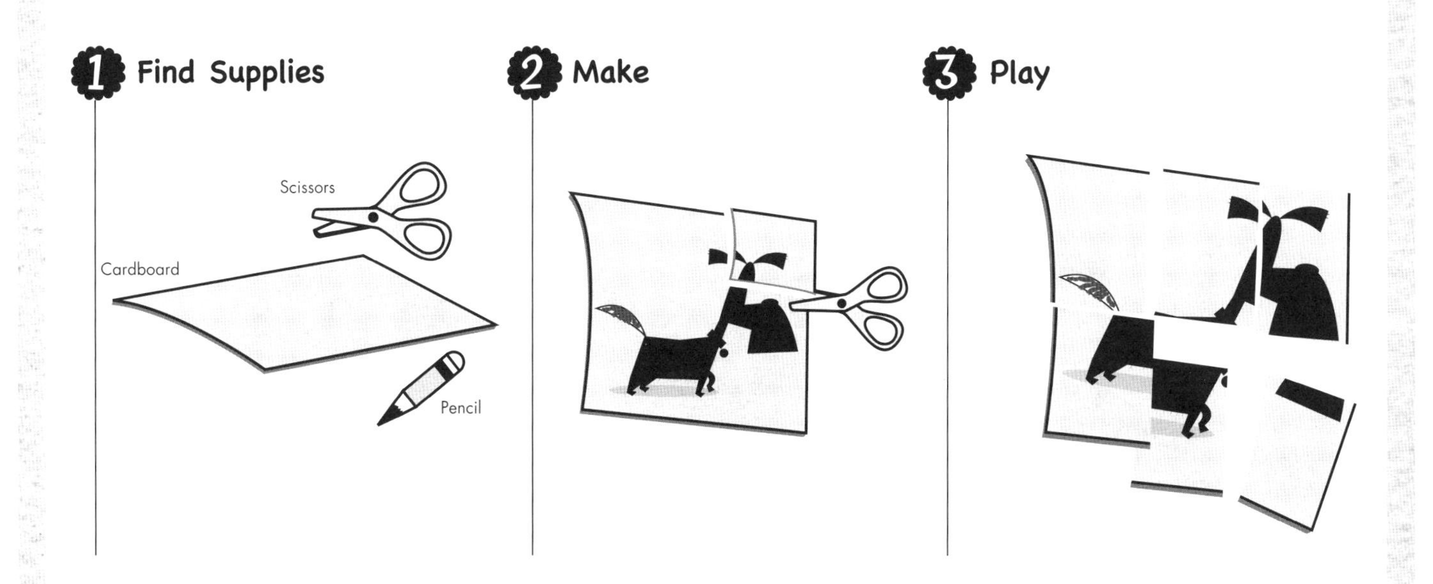

Will it Fit?

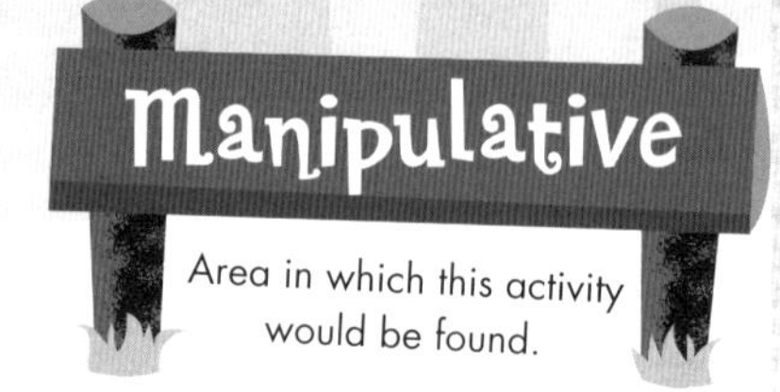

Materials

- ❑ Variety of found objects (bottle caps, plastic, lids, toilet paper tubes)
- ❑ Different sized rocks and sticks
- ❑ 3 different sized cups or containers basket

Activity Description

- Place all the various found objects from your room or outdoors in a basket. (spoon, pencil, stick, book...)
- Children choose an object and try to fit it inside one of the cups.
- If the object fits inside a cup they lay it next to that cup and then choose a new object to try.
- Children continue until they have experimented with all objects.

Extension Idea

Set out many of the same object, and encourage children to fill each cup with the objects and count how many objects fit in each cup. Which cup holds the most? The least?

Scoop it Out

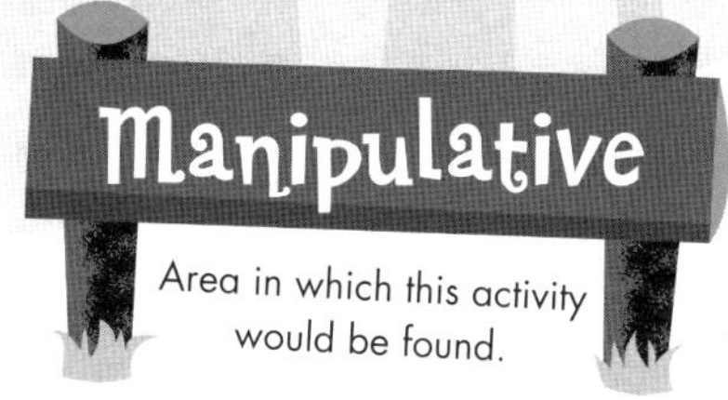

Skills
- Literacy
- Coordination/fine motor
- Directional awareness

Materials
- ❑ 2 Bowls
- ❑ Pebbles or dry beans
- ❑ Spoon or large seed cut in half

Activity Description
- Place two bowls side by side.
- Fill the bowl to the left with all the pebbles.
- Children scoop spoonfuls of beans from left to right.
- Child can decide to move half, a quarter or all of the pebbles to the other bowl.

Extension Idea

See if children can pick-up and move one pebble at a time.

Make a Library

Reading

Area in which this activity would be found.

Skills

- Fine motor
- Creative expression
- Emerging writing

Materials

- ☐ Flat surface for drawing & writing
- ☐ Something to write with and/or plant dye
- ☐ Sharp instrument for poking a hole
- ☐ Sturdy string/thread/leather

Activity Description

- Children make individual books or work together to make books.
- Children draw pictures and write or dictate story for teacher to write.
- Punch holes and assemble book.
- Place on your library bookshelf.

1 Find Supplies

2 Make

3 Read

Extension Idea

Work together as a class to make a story. The teacher asks the first child a question such as, "How does the story begin?" Child dictates while teacher writes. Teacher then asks the next child, "Then what happens?" Child dictates and teacher writes on a new piece of paper. Teacher continues until each child has contributed. Children decorate pages and teacher binds the class book.

Draw the Story

Skills
- Sequencing
- Memory
- Group interaction

Materials
- ☐ Flat surface for drawing (paper or bark)
- ☐ Something to write with
- ☐ Old clothes, hats, shoes

Activity Description
- Ask children to describe a simple scene (A man goes to the market). Teacher draws a simple sketch of this scene.
- Ask what happens next. Continue to draw each idea until there are 3-4 sequential story pictures.
- Show pictures to children.
- Children play with cards and put them in sequential order and retell story.
- Children draw their own story cards.

Extension Idea

Children use the ideas on the cards to create a play and set up props and costumes in the dramatic play area.

A-Maze-Ing

Reading/Writing

Area in which this activity would be found.

Skills

- Emerging writing
- Fine motor

Materials

- ☐ Cardboard pieces
- ☐ Stick
- ☐ Something to write with

Activity Description

- Draw a long zig-zag, curve, loop, or diagonal line from the top of the cardboard pieces to the bottom.
- Set out all the cardboard mazes.
- Children hold a stick or use their finger and follow the line from beginning to end until they get through the maze.
- Encourage children to draw their own mazes and share them with friends.

1 Make or Find Supplies

2 Play

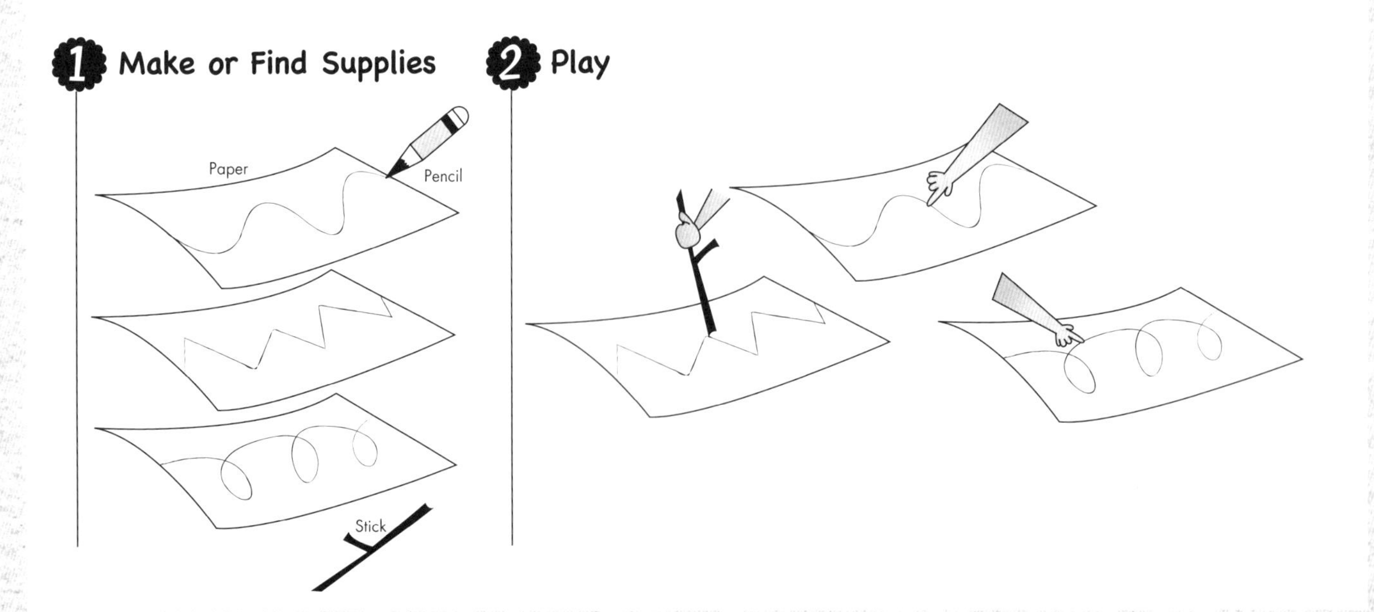

Letter Code

Skills
- Drawing
- Letter recognition
- Phonetic awareness

Materials
- ☐ Paper
- ☐ Something to write with
- ☐ Rocks

Activity Description
- Children think of an animal or object they would like to draw.
- Say the word together aloud and identify which letter that animal or object begins with. Write the letter on a stone.
- Children match their picture with the letter stone.
- Place all drawings in one pile and letter rocks in another. Children choose 2-3 pictures and try to find the matching rocks.

Extension Idea

Have children draw their name using the same method as described above. If your name is Sue, you may draw a snake, umbrella, and elephant!

Silly Mix & Match Book

Skills
- Drawing
- Writing
- Critical thinking

Materials
- ☐ 5 pieces of paper
- ☐ Something to write with
- ☐ String

Activity Description

- Draw a line across each piece of paper in the same place.
- Children draw a person or animal on each paper with the head above the line and the body below the line.
- Punch holes and tie the pages together. Carefully cut all the pages on the line.
- Children open books and decide which silly head and body combination they want to create.
- Tip: It is fine if the child scribbles or does not keep the head above the line. It is still fun to mix and match the pictures.

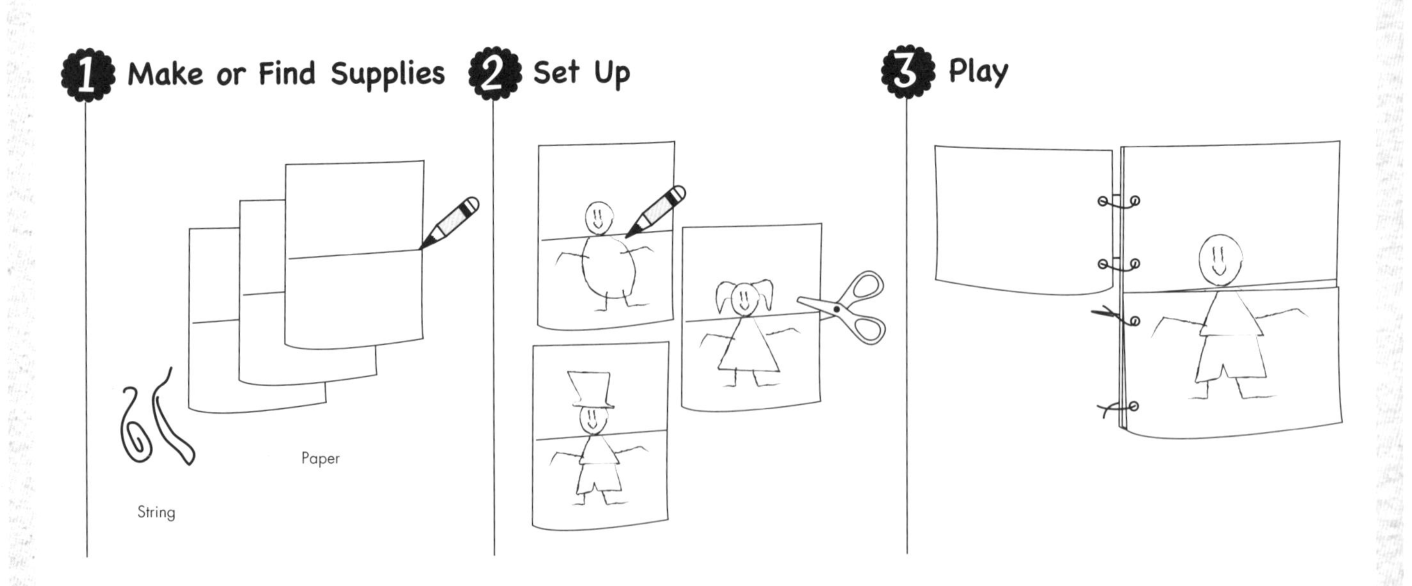

Letter Pointer Hunt

Reading

Area in which this activity would be found.

Skills

- Alphabetic awareness
- Fluency
- Visual discrimination

Materials

- ☐ Cardboard
- ☐ Scissors
- ☐ Something to write with
- ☐ Books or printed materials

Activity Description

- Cut small arrows out of cardboard
- Print a single letter on each pointer (arrow).
- Children choose a pointer and go on a letter hunt.
- Children look at the words in books and around the room for the letter. Children touch the letter with the pointer.

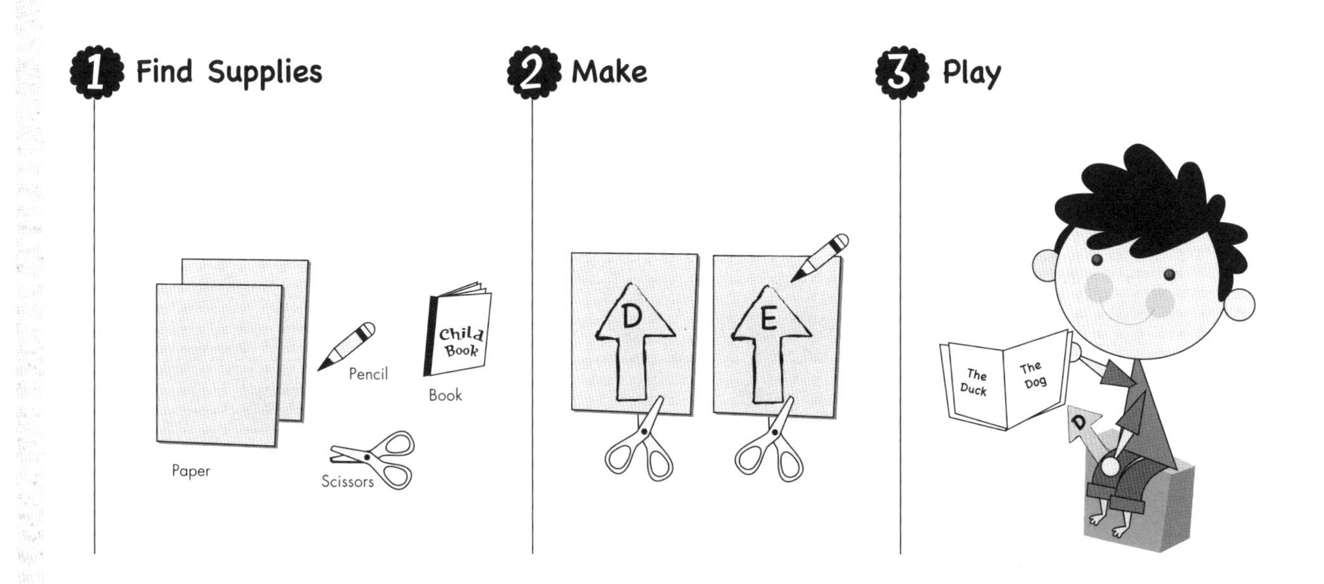

Number Memory Stones

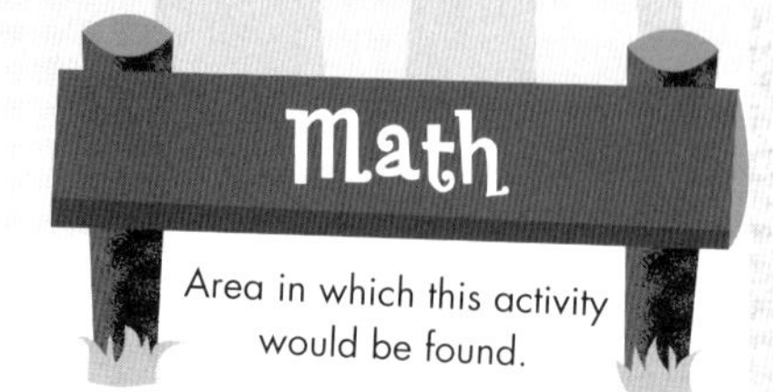

Skills

- Number recognition
- Counting
- Memory and matching

Materials
- ☐ 20 stones
- ☐ Something to write with

Activity Description

- Label 10 stones with the numerals 0-9.
- Label another 10 stones with dots equaling 0-9.
- Place the stones on the ground, numeral and dot side down.
- Children take turns turning over two stones. If the two stones match with the numeral and dot quantity, it's a winner! Child picks up and keeps the stones. If they do not match, child turns them back over.

Circle Pieces

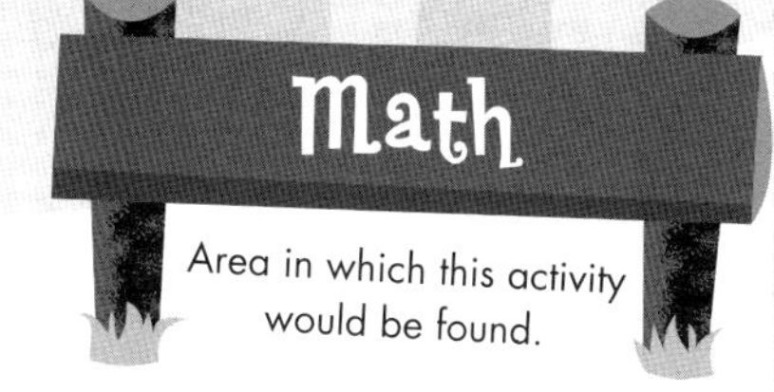

Skills
- Spatial awareness
- Fine motor

Materials
- ❑ Paper (new or used)
- ❑ Scissors (or cutting tool)
- ❑ Basket

Activity Description
- Cut or tear out 10 equal sized paper circles all the same size.
- Take 6 of the circles and cut them all in half.
- Take 6 of the halves, and cut them in half again to make quarters.
- Take 6 of the quarters and cut them in half to create eighths.
- Children use the different sized pieces and lay them on top of a whole circle.
- Children see how many different ways they can cover the circle

Extension Idea

Try the same activity but cut out 10 squares, diamonds, or octagons.

Number Matching

Math

Area in which this activity would be found.

Skills
- Counting
- One-to-one correspondence
- Number recognition

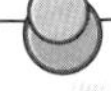

Materials
- ☐ 2 bowls or baskets
- ☐ 10 small objects
- ☐ 10 number pieces (any paper or flat object to draw or paint numbers on)

Activity Description
- Write numbers 1-10 on a strip of paper.
- Place number pieces in bowl or basket.
- Place 10 small objects in another bowl or basket.
- Children choose a number piece and count out the same amount of small objects.

Estimation Jars

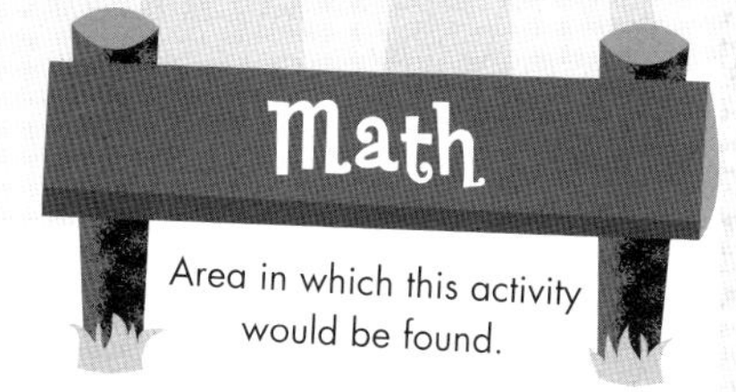

Skills
- Logic
- Estimation
- Fine motor

Materials
- ☐ Jar or clear bottle
- ☐ Leaves, seeds, or sticks
- ☐ Something to write with
- ☐ Paper/something to write on.

Activity Description
- Fill a jar with handfuls of a single type of object (such as leaves, sticks, pebbles or seeds).
- Without touching, children take turns looking into the jar and guessing how many objects are inside the jar.
- Help children record their estimations.
- Teacher and children count the contents together.

Invent a Shape

Math

Area in which this activity would be found.

Skills

- Counting
- Geometry
- Fine motor

Materials

- ☐ Small pieces of wood or cardboard
- ☐ Dirt or sand surface

Activity Description

- Children take any number of wood or cardboard pieces and arrange them in a design on a dirt floor or in a sand box.
- Children use their fingers to trace around the wood pieces in the dirt.
- Count the pieces of wood used to make the finished design.
- Remove the pieces of wood and look at the shape in the dirt.

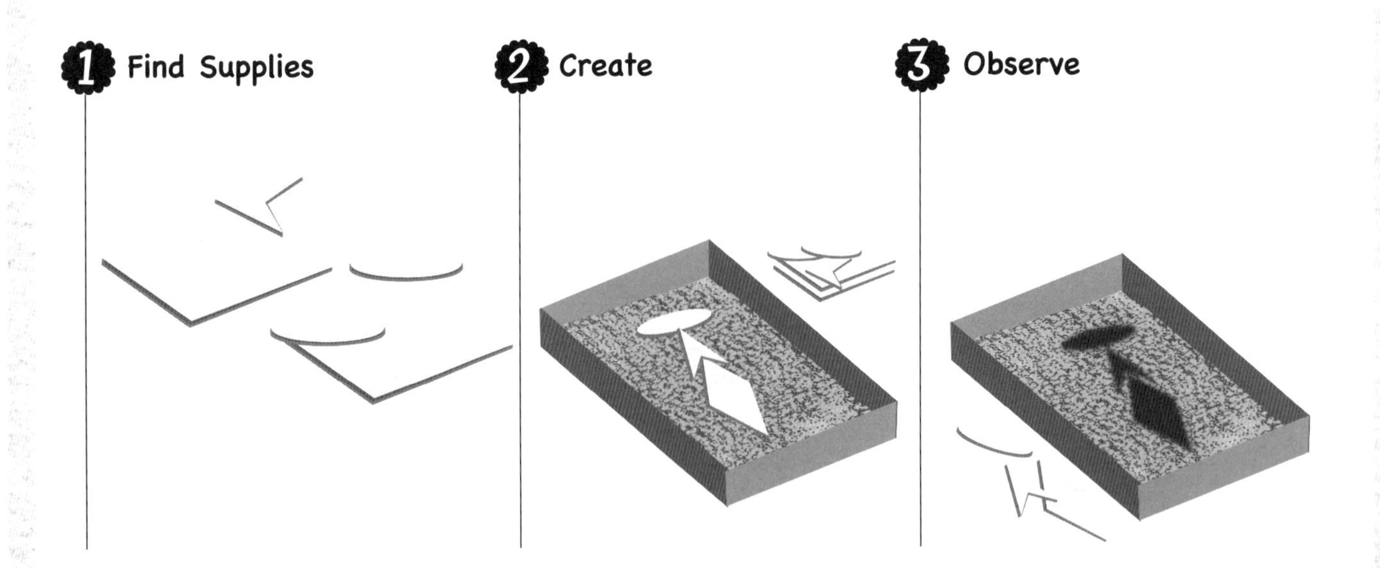

Square Collage

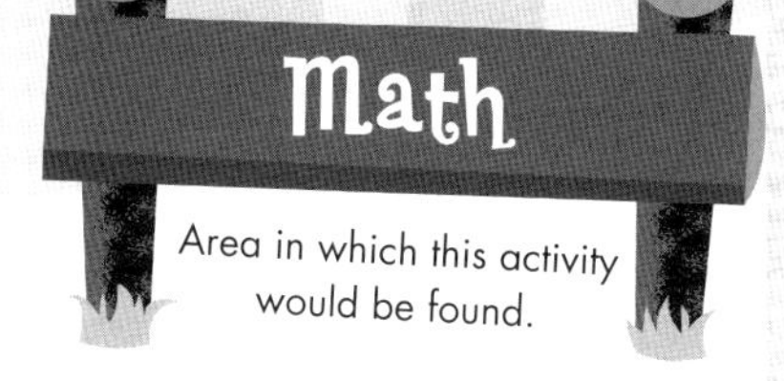

Skills
- Shapes
- Fine motor
- Critical thinking

Materials
- ❑ Fabric
- ❑ Paper or Cardboard
- ❑ Scissors

Activity Description
- Cut out different sizes of squares from various textures. (fabric, paper, cardboard, tree bark)
- Children make square collages by arranging the squares onto a large square piece of paper.
- Do not glue so children can make designs over and over.

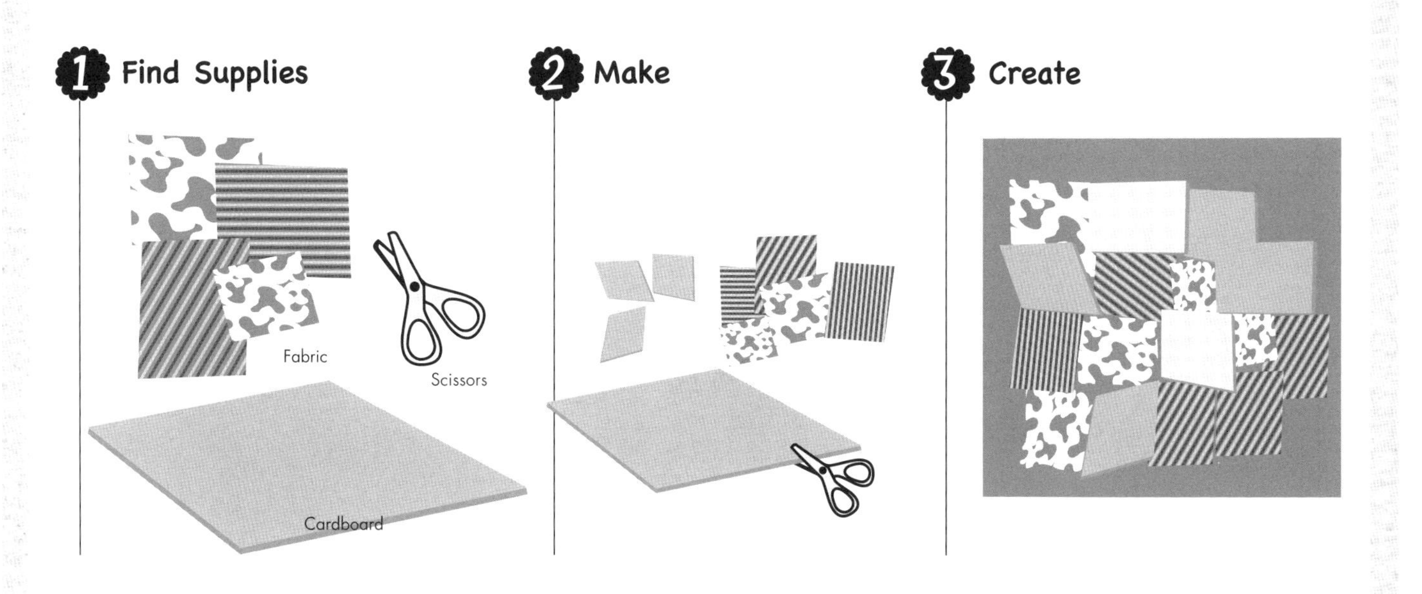

Sticks, Squares & Rectangles

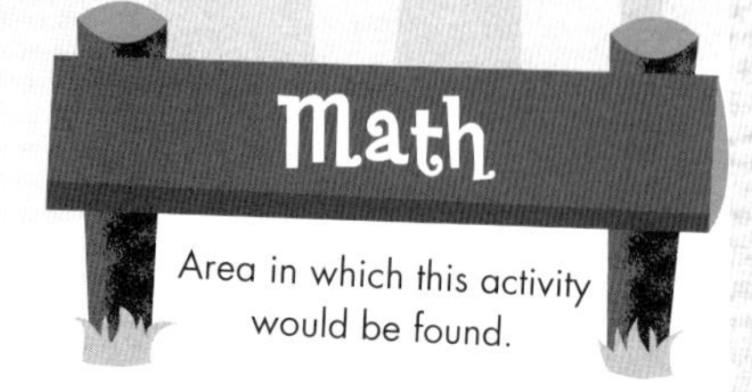

Skills
- Measurement
- Shapes
- Fine Motor

Materials
- ☐ Sticks
- ☐ Sand/ dirt

Activity Description
- Break sticks into two sizes: short and long.
- Children choose 4 equally sized sticks and lay them on the dirt or sand to make a square.
- Children press down on each stick to make an imprint in the dirt. Carefully lift the sticks and trace the imprint with finger or another stick.

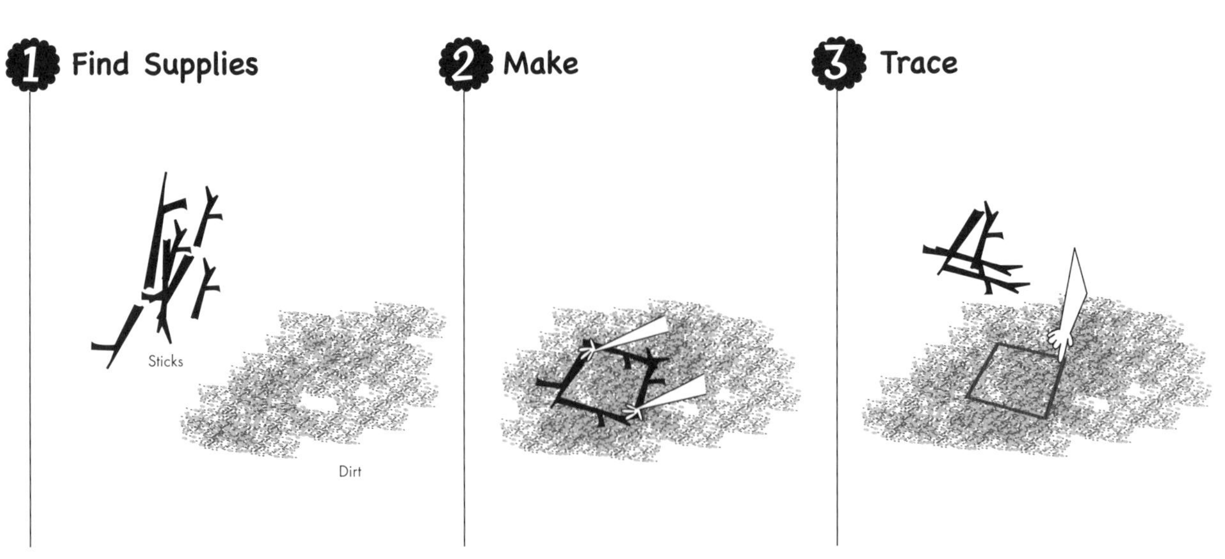

Extension Idea

Repeat activity but try to make a rectangle.

Number Tiles

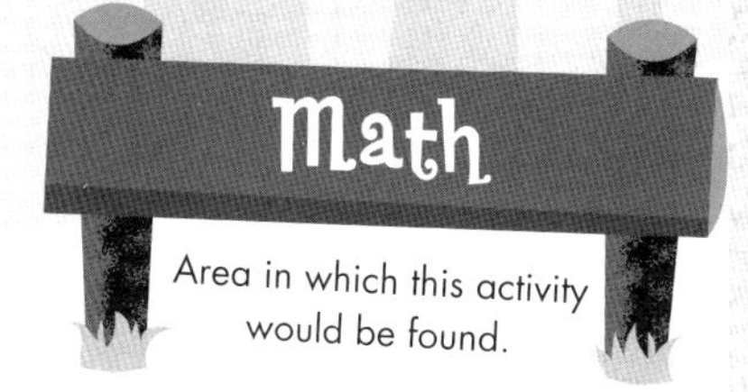

Skills

- Number recognition
- Counting
- Matching

Materials

- ☐ Cardboard or paper
- ☐ Something to write with
- ☐ Basket or box
- ☐ Scissors

Activity Description

- Cut or tear 10 rectangle cards and 10 square cards.
- Draw a line down the middle of each rectangle card. Label one side of the line on the rectangle card with numerals 1-10. Label the square cards with dots from 1-10.
- Child draws a card from the basket. If the card matches either the numeral or quantity of dots, they lay down the card next to the match.
- Continue until all the cards are connected or no more matches can be found.

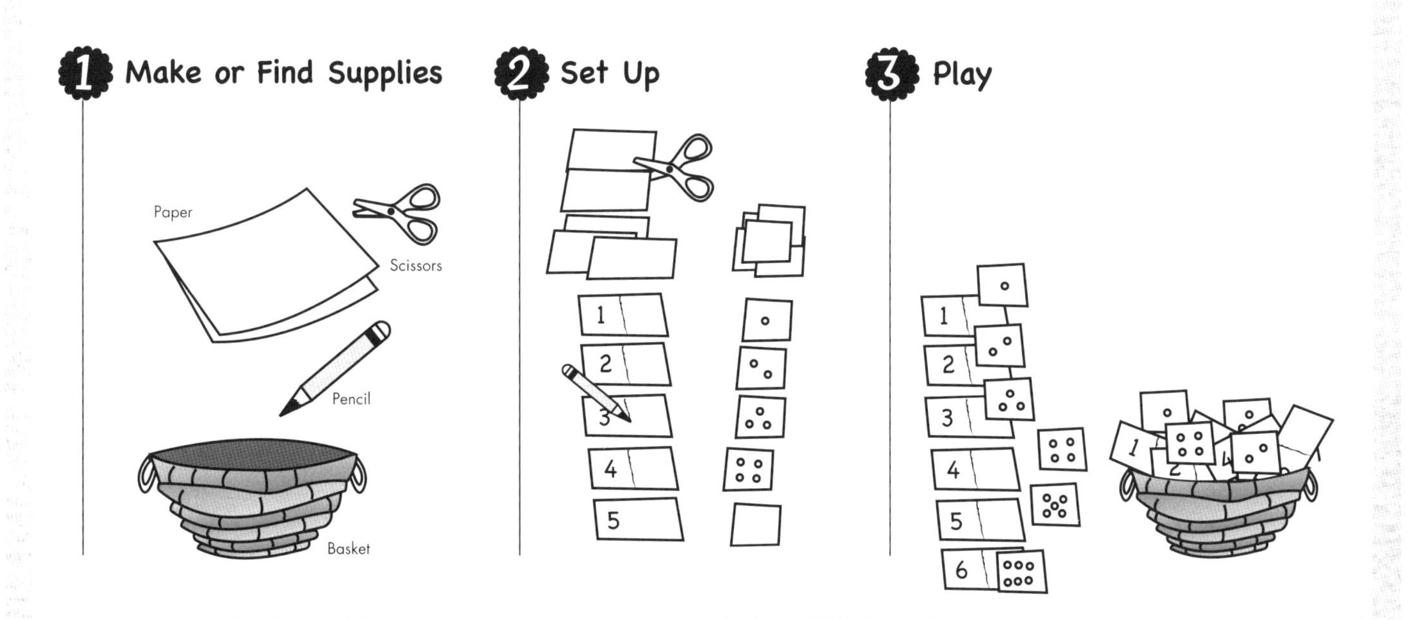

Look at Me

Circle Time

Area in which this activity would be found.

Skills
- Self-esteem
- Oral language
- Fine motor

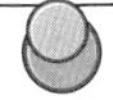

Materials
- ☐ Paper
- ☐ Something to write with

Activity Description

- Give each child a piece of paper.
- Encourage the children to draw a picture of themselves as a baby on one side of the paper.
- Children draw a picture of themselves as they are today on the other side of the paper.
- Sit in a circle and children take turns showing and telling about their drawings.
- Optional: If you have a mirror or reflective surface, set it out for children to use during this activity.

I'm Proud

Skills

- Self acceptance/self esteem
- Social emotional development

Activity Description

- Invite one child to sit in the middle of the circle or stand up in the classroom as the focus person.
- Have the focus person make an "I'm proud" statement.

  Examples:
  "I am proud that I am..."
  "I am proud that I am able to..."
- Have other children give positive feedback or statements of appreciation to the focus person.
- Continue the process until each child has a turn being the focus person.

Feelings are Okay

Circle Time

Area in which this activity would be found.

Skills
- Self awareness
- Phonemic awareness

Materials
- ☐ Paper
- ☐ Something to write with

Activity Description

- On paper or a chalkboard, draw different faces – happy, sad, excited, tired, angry, etc.
- Ask children to look at the different faces and decide which face looks most like how they feel at that moment.
- As the teacher, explain your feelings first to model the activity.
- Go around the circle, giving each child an opportunity to point or touch the face that represents his/her feelings. Allow time for each child that is able to use words to describe his/her feelings.
- Everyone says this rhyme together after each child has a turn.

1 Make & Find Supplies

2 Find your Feeling

3 Say the Rhyme

Sometimes I feel happy,
sometimes I feel sad
Sometimes I feel lonely,
sometimes I feel glad
I am me everyday, my
feelings are okay.

I Am Special

Skills
- Self awareness
- Oral communication

Art, Circle Time

Area in which this activity would be found.

Materials
- ☐ Paper
- ☐ Tape
- ☐ Scissors
- ☐ Something to write with

Activity Description

- Trace each child's hand onto a piece of paper and cut out the hands.
- Cut out a tree trunk shape from paper and tape it on the wall.
- Invite each child to complete the following sentence: "I am special because..."
- As children dictate, teacher writes their response on their hand.
- Invite children to tape their leaf (hand cut-out) anywhere on the tree trunk.
- Stand together under the new tree and sing (to the tune of Mary had a little Lamb)

I'm as special as I can be
I can be, I can be
I'm as special as I can be
There's no one just like me

Who & what is Missing?

Skills
- Reasoning
- Cooperation
- Visual discrimination

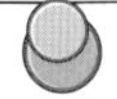

Materials
- ☐ Variety of objects
- ☐ Tray

Activity Description

Missing Friends:
- Sit in a circle on the floor and work together to identify which children are missing or not present today.
- Say the name of each missing child and blow kisses in the air for the child.

Missing Objects:
- Collect 3-7 different objects: for example a nut, rock, shell, twig, coin, pencil, bottle cap.
- Lay all objects on a tray or table and invite children to view the objects but not to touch them.
- Secretly, remove one object from the tray. Announce to the children that an object is missing. "Look and see, something is missing, what could it be?"
- Children view the tray and try to determine what is missing.
- Children take turns guessing. Teacher gives hints.

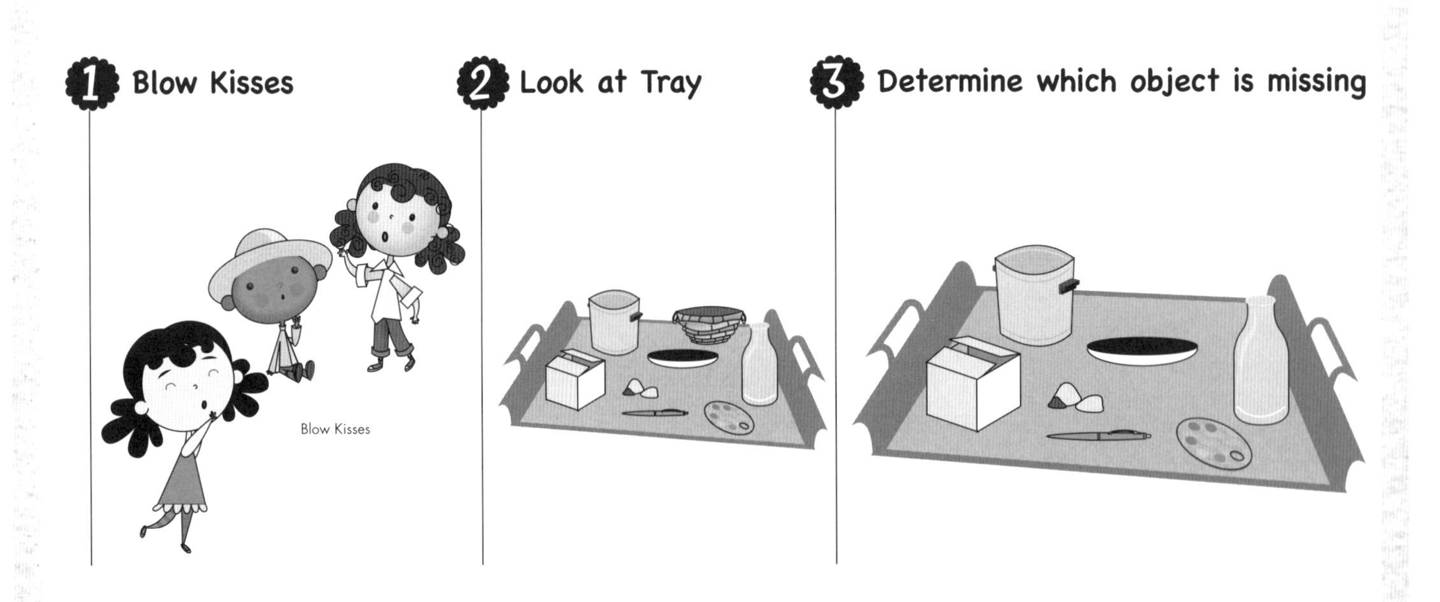

Casting Bad Feelings

Circle Time

Area in which this activity would be found.

Skills
- Sense of community
- Self-awareness
- Positive group interaction

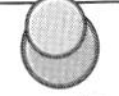

Materials
- ☐ Paper or cardboard
- ☐ Something to write with
- ☐ Old box, envelope or bag

Activity Description
- Have each child share a hurtful feeling or behavior he or she never wants to hear or see again. Teacher writes the feelings on separate pieces of paper.
- Take the children outside and throw the box away.
- Have all children say goodbye to the bad feelings
- Ask children what they could do to help each other feel good and keep the bad feelings away.

Tangle

Circle Time

Area in which this activity would be found.

Skills

- Problem-solving
- Teamwork skills
- Gross Motor

Note

- Activity for children 5 years or older.

Activity Description

- All children stand in a circle facing inward.
- Teacher asks children to put one hand behind their back until told otherwise.
- Teacher asks children to "reach across the circle with your free hand and grab the hand of someone not next to you."
- Each child is holding one other player's hand, still with the other hand behind the back.
- Teacher reminds children NOT to let go of the other player's hand no matter what!
- Teacher asks children to "bring out the hand behind your back, reach across the circle and grasp the free hand of someone else."
- The group will be all tangled up.
- Teacher invites children to untangle without letting go of hands.
- It is alright if children end up facing outward in the resulting circle.

1 Reach across circle and hold hands

2 Untangle without letting go

Note: Children will have to step through other's gaps, or over their arms or legs in complicated ways. Often several linked maneuvers are necessary to make any progress.

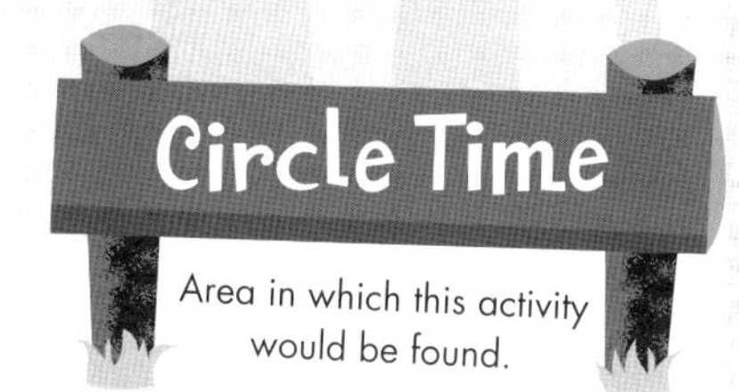

Skills

- Reasoning
- Cooperation
- Body control
- Auditory discrimination

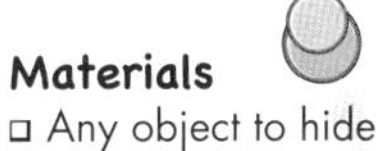

Materials

- ☐ Any object to hide

Activity Description

- Children sit in circle. Invite one child to be the treasure hunter. This child closes his/her eyes.
- Hide the object somewhere in the room.
- The treasure hunter opens his/her eyes and begins walking around the room in search of the object.
- As the hunter searches, the other children give clapping clues. Children clap softly if the hunter is far away from the object. As the hunter moves closer to the object, the children clap louder and faster.
- Continue clapping until the hunter finds the object.

Note: Let's work together and help each other reach our goals.

Guess Who?

Circle Time

Area in which this activity would be found.

Skills

- Memory
- Group participation
- Verbalizing names

Materials

- ❑ One large sheet, towel, blanket, or piece of cloth

Activity Description

- Before playing the game children should try to memorize each other's names. Sit or stand in a circle and share names.
- Divide children into two groups.
- Half of the children stand on one side of the sheet. The rest, stand on the other side.
- Children quickly choose one person from their group to move up close to the sheet.
- When each group has chosen one child, count to 3 and then drop the sheet. The two children standing call out the other person's name as quickly as possible, if they can remember!
- Each child who guesses correctly gets one point for their team. Game can be played without points as well.
- The teacher then holds the sheet back up and groups select a new person to stand up close to the sheet
- The game goes on as long as children are interested, or until all names are learned.

1 Children stand behind sheet.

2 Say name of new friend.

Note: Intended for groups of children who are learning each other's names

Make a Square

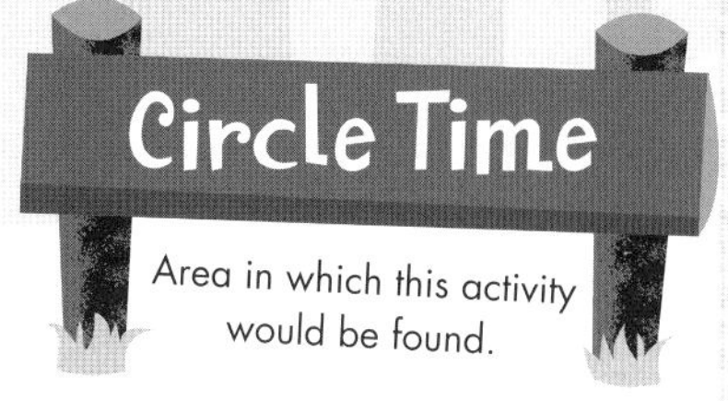

Skills
- Shapes
- Problem-solving
- Gross Motor

Materials
- ❑ Tape or string

Activity Description
- Use tape or string to make a square shape in the group time area.
- Invite the children to sit on the tape in a square for group time.
- Discuss what makes a square a square (4 equal sides).
- Show the children pictures of squares.
- Encourage the children to look around the classroom and point out objects that are square.
- Organize children into groups of four and challenge them to make squares, circles or other shapes with their bodies.